AS A MAN THINKETH

Jonathan Brown

As a Man Thinketh

"Mind is the master power that molds and makes,
And man is mind, and evermore he takes
The tool of thought, and, shaping what he wills,
Brings forth a thousand joys, a thousand ills: -
He thinks in secret, and it comes to pass:
Environment is but his looking glass."
~ James Allen ~

"The mind is its own place, and in itself can make a
heaven of hell, a hell of heaven."
~ John Milton, Paradise Lost ~

Contents

Preface

"The wind extinguishes a candle but energises a fire.
You want to be a fire and wish for the wind."
Nassim Taleb [1]

I have felt like a candle in danger of being extinguished by the wind. I have felt frail and weak in the face of a storm and, while I can still experience life this way, I have also learnt to grow, add substance and foundation, and access within me a bonfire where before there was only a single flame. This book is the story of my journey from candle to fire, from fear of being extinguished to developing strength.

I first heard of 'As a Man Thinketh'[2] while working through an anxiety disorder that I had developed in my mid-twenties. For one reason or another, an event in my life had triggered an anxious response and, unfortunately, feelings of shame regarding both the stimulus and my resulting anxiety caused me to hide the symptoms that I was experiencing. This wasn't a good choice and much like a physical injury that deteriorates when left untreated, my anxiety worsened. Luckily one day, while listening to a podcast, the host mentioned 'As a Man Thinketh, describing it as one of the most influential self-help/self-development books ever written. I downloaded a copy of the book that day and began my recovery through engagement with the ideas.

Now, I want to be honest and say that some ideas and vocabulary in 'As a Man Thinketh' cause me trouble. Some of the language (such as 'good', 'bad' and 'righteous') invites judgement, which is not helpful within a therapeutic setting, some of the imagery and vocabulary is somewhat outdated, and, as a person of faith, I feel at times an overreliance on self for redemption, where I believe divine help is required. However, it is worth looking past these obstacles and presenting the core ideas.

To help with this, I have modernised the language somewhat and divided the original book into 37 short chapters (I have included the full original manuscript at the end of the book should you wish to read this). I hope to produce an easy book to engage with, offering digestible chunks of information. Another key addition is the inclusion of questions for reflection and specific actions for the reader to undertake. In the journey to health – be that physical, emotional and/or mental – information alone is not enough, actions matter! As such, I would encourage you to read this book slowly, taking time to engage with the questions and deliberately working through the suggested activities.

As you work your way through the chapters, I hope that you will begin to experience concrete changes in your life.

Lastly, it's ok if you are still a candle and not yet a bonfire – you are still alight! The stars appear as tiny specs of light within the infinite blackness of the sky and yet we still wonder at their beauty.

1. As a Man Thinketh

"To realise that you are not your thoughts is when you begin to awaken spiritually."
~ Eckhart Tolle [1] ~

As a Man Thinketh

I clearly remember an important moment in my journey to recovery from an anxiety disorder. I was meeting with an educational psychologist to discuss the needs of a particular child in my school when, during this conversation, the educational psychologist mentioned that a common symptom of anxiety is unwanted and unpleasant thoughts. This idea – that we are not our thoughts – grabbed me, as I could see a path out of anxiety within it.

I was plagued by unwanted and unpleasant thoughts that provoked an extremely anxious response. At times, I felt like most of my brain was engaged in anxious thinking, leaving little head space and emotional energy for anything else. I was concerned about what these thoughts said about me as a person. So, the idea that these thoughts were not 'me' was a lifeline.

In the coming pages, we will explore the role our thinking has on our feelings and behaviours and better understand the influence that feelings and behaviours can have on thinking and one another!

My mum, a doctor in counselling psychology, once described thoughts as the pop-up ads that appear on your computer screen. These ads are produced through various algorithms that try and put information in front of you – "You need a new pair of running shoes? Here you go!" – but they don't always get it right! The ads can pop up at an unwanted time, can pop up too frequently, can offer products we aren't interested in and can be irrelevant, unconnected to you and potentially dangerous to engage with ("Do you want to earn thousands by working at home? Click here and find out how!"). As we use the internet, we develop our ability to filter the various ads that pop up on our screen, select useful ads, ignore unwanted ones, and deal appropriately with content we think might be harmful. Interestingly, navigating these pop-ups doesn't produce an emotional response within me (other than the occasional annoyance) – I don't worry about what kind of person I must be because my computer shows me ads about teeth whiteners, diets, or singles in my area.

Eckhart Tolle wisely suggests that "rather than being your thoughts and emotions, be the awareness behind them"[2]. You are not the pop-up adverts – you are the observer that notices them!

Take a deep breath and read that again!

A second helpful, although perhaps slightly more daunting idea is that while we are not our thoughts, we may become them.

In our digital world, we are familiar with the idea of programming. Our devices run on the programmes written for them; they work as instructed, their actions are not spontaneous but the natural outworking of the instructions and commands within their programmes. Similarly, our lives run on our thoughts and the stories we tell.

What does this mean for us today? It means we aren't our thoughts and that our thoughts play an important role in framing our experience and informing us as a person. Think about it like this; while pop-up ads are present and available, it is how you interact with these ads that will shape your online experience and affect your computer's performance. If the way you are interacting with these ads isn't giving you the results you are looking for, you can change. If interacting and engaging with thoughts aren't giving you the results you want, you can change!

"To realise that you are not your thoughts is when you begin to awaken spiritually."
~ Eckhart Tolle ~

Consider:

- How much attention do you give your thought life? For example, how would you describe the overall tone of your thought life?

....

....

....

....

....

....

....

- To what extent could your thoughts be shaping your current experience?

....

....

....

....

....

....

....

- What effects have your thoughts had on your development as a person?

....

....

....

....

....

....

....

Actions:

Our thoughts can often occur just outside of our awareness. Today try and notice the thoughts you are thinking and be curious about them.

Ask yourself questions like:

- *Do I believe the thought I am thinking?*

- *How is thinking this thought making me feel?*

- *What different thoughts could I think?*

"By far the most vital lesson I have ever learned is the importance of what we think...
Our thoughts make us what we are."
~ Dale Carnegie [3] ~

2. The Good Person

"...it does take 10 years to be an overnight success."
~ Miki Agrawal [1] ~

The Good Person

As humans, laws govern us, and we can't trick these laws or avoid their natural consequences. Just so, becoming a 'good person' is not the result of chance or favourable circumstance but is the natural result of a continued effort to improve our thinking quality.

It is often said that we become like those that we spend time with. Likewise, we become our thoughts. To become a 'good person', we must spend time in the presence of good thoughts, thoughts of patience, compassion, thankfulness and forgiveness. However, indulging, accepting, and cultivating negative and harmful thoughts will damage a person's character.

Consider:

In his book, 'Bounce: The Myth of Talent and the Power of Practice'[2], author Matthew Syed argues there are no natural geniuses, only people who have worked in a focused and deliberate way to develop and improve. One example he gives to support this claim is a 1991 study by Florida State University psychologist Anders Ericsson who undertook an extensive investigation into the cause of outstanding performance at the Music Academy of West Berlin[3].

Based on the assessments of professors from the Music Academy and objective measures such as success in open competitions, Ericsson and his team organised their focus group of students into three categories: Outstanding, Extremely Good and Least Able.

Once the students had been grouped, Ericsson and his team undertook in-depth biographical interviews with all students, seeking to identify what caused the outstanding students to be the better musicians, considering elements such as musical parents and access to tutors and musical programmes.

After extensive research, Ericsson's findings pointed to one key distinguishing feature, the outstanding students worked harder! Ericsson discovered that by the age of twenty, students in the 'Outstanding' group had, on average, practised for around 10 000 hours. This was 2000 hours more than the 'Extremely Good' group and 6000 hours more than the 'Least Able' group.

After noticing this trend, Ericsson and his team ran further checks to validate their findings and discovered that none of the 'Outstanding' players had achieved their ranking without the additional hours of practice. In addition, no students had accrued the hours of practice but not risen to the higher ability groups.

It is easy to think that some people 'have it made', but it's neither true nor helpful. The myth of talent would rob us of a better future by convincing us that effort isn't required. *"Becoming a 'good person' is not the result of chance or favourable circumstance but is the natural result of continued effort in right thinking."*

Questions:

- What might be the unintended consequences of believing in 'favourable circumstance' rather than 'continued effort in improving the quality of our thinking'?

....

....

....

....

....

....

....

- If you chose your thoughts, what would they be?

....

....

....

....

....

....

Actions:

Choose three to five thoughts you would like to be your most common thoughts. This could be specific thoughts or themes, such as generosity, thankfulness, or patience. The phrasing of these thoughts is important, avoiding judgement and/or feelings of blame. A simple way to check on the phrasing of your thoughts is to look for a wagging finger. By this, I mean you should look at the thought you have written down and consider whether a strict parent could say this as they wag their finger at you. Consider the following as an example:

You desire to worry less, so you write down the thought 'I will not worry'. While a good starting point, this thought can feed your inner critic, pointing out the occasions you have fallen short. This thought is also negatively framed, such that your focus is on the thing you are trying not to do. This thought can be improved by considering instead what you are aiming for; in this instance, you may want to change 'I will not worry' to 'I can choose peace'.

Wear something today that will remind you of these thoughts and try to think them. This isn't about blame, shame or judgement, so when you notice these aren't the thoughts you are thinking, gently move towards them.

Create a mantra, or short phrase to 'spend more time' in the presence of well-chosen thoughts. Here are a few ideas to get you started:

- *'I can choose peace'*
- *'I can be calm'*
- *'I am loved'*
- *'I am valuable'*
- *'I am strong'*
- *'I can choose to rest'*
- *'I am thankful for...'*
- *'I can choose what I focus on'*

....

....

....

....

....

"A man is but the product of his thoughts,
what he thinks he becomes."
~ Mahatma Gandhi [3] ~

3. The Master & Moulder

"True independence of character empowers us to act rather than be acted upon."
~ Steven Covey [1] ~

The Master & Moulder

We build ourselves up or tear ourselves down in our minds. We have the abilities to either destroy ourselves or create a life of peace, stability and joy.

By thinking well and surrounding ourselves with well-chosen thoughts, we can rise above the worst aspects of our character and display the likeness of the divine within us. We lose ourselves and become far less than we were meant to be by thinking poorly.

Between these two poles of thinking, we find all grades of character, and in every kind, we are the maker and master of ourselves. We reap what we sow.

In this truth, we find something fierce and beautiful; the power to change! You are the captain of your ship, the moulder of your character and the maker and shaper of your environment and destiny.

In you, there is the intelligence and love required to unlock every situation so that, for you, it is a blessing. Within you is the power to transform not only yourself but the world. Is it bitter or sweet, harmful or strengthening, setting you back or building you up – in your mind, you make it so!

Consider:

Reflecting on this passage, I am reminded of the saying 'Everybody wants to go to heaven, but nobody wants to die!". It is normal to desire better, yet how willing are we to work to achieve our goal? We can find ourselves busy with the business of doing everything but the work. We collect knowledge, strategies and examples, but the change doesn't come from knowing. It comes from doing, from applying knowing. Entrepreneur Derek Sivers wisely reminds us that "if more information was the answer, we would all be millionaires with perfect abs!" [2]

Taking responsibility for our lives through deliberate action can feel daunting, yet it is ultimately liberating; we can live our lives instead of being lived by the lives of others.

Steven Covey offers an interesting take on the word 'responsibility', he presents it as response-ability; our ability to choose our response. We all can choose how we will respond in different situations. When we interact with a situation, we can find a gap between what it offers us and how we respond to it. We can choose grace, despite being offered frustration; we can choose peace, despite being offered distress.

In his book 'Man's Search for Meaning' [3], Victor Frankl writes of his experience of cleaning out one of the gas chambers following a mass execution. He recounts being in the cell, tired and near starved to death, undertaking the truly horrific work of cleaning the very room where countless Jews had been murdered, when he had the following revelation:

"The last of the human freedoms: to choose one's attitude in any given set of circumstances, to choose one's own way. And there were always choices to make. Every day, every hour, offered the opportunity to make a decision, a decision which determined whether you would or would not submit to those powers which threatened to rob you of your very self, your inner freedom; which determined whether or not you become the plaything to circumstance, renouncing freedom and dignity... Between stimulus and response is the freedom to choose."

In the gas chambers, it appears possible to choose our response.

Questions:

Think of a situation where your response is not serving you well. Reflecting on your 'response-ability', consider what kind of response you would be happy with or serve you better?

- *What would be the first steps to achieve this?*

....

....

....

....

....

....

....

- *What obstacles might you have to overcome?*

....

....

....

....

....

....

....

- *How will you do this?*

....

....

....

....

....

....

....

- *What else might help you achieve this goal?*

....

....

....

....

....

....

....

*"True independence of character empowers us to act
rather than be acted upon."*
~ Steven Covey ~

4. Good Steward/Bad Steward

"Easy to, easy not to."
~ Jim Rohn [1] ~

Good Steward/Bad Steward

We are always in control. Even in our poorest state, we still retain the power to change, but in our poor state, we are like neglectful stewards who have misgoverned the estates left to them.

Yet, we need not remain this way. We can recognise the law governing our present state through honest reflection and thought, that being 'reaping and sowing'. In finding and accepting this truth, we can become like the good steward able to direct his power and energy towards building up and flourishing.

Thus, the issue is that we become 'conscious masters.' We must bring into our consciousness the ideas, beliefs, rules, and assumptions shaping the thoughts within us and consider whether these are seeds we wish to continue sowing.

Consider

Everything is a seed! There is no such thing as seedless thought or seedless action, everything is a seed and everything will bring forth. The challenge is to plant seeds of our choosing consciously.

This truth appears so simple when stated like this, so why is it so hard to achieve? Why is it so hard to consistently and consciously sow good seed?

Jim Rohn used a phrase that perfectly sums up this issue – 'easy to and easy not to'. Jim often taught that success is nothing more than a few simple habits practised every day. The habits, he argued, are easy to do. The problem is, they are also easy *not* to do!

Let me give you an example. I had major spinal surgery as a teenager and now need to do yoga every day to stay flexile and pain-free. This is easy to do because it's something I can achieve without anyone else's help or any additional resources. The problem is, it's also very easy not to do my 10-minute routine in the morning! But notice this, not doing my morning yoga is still planting a seed for by the end of the week, my back is tight and sore.

I sowed a seed; I harvest its fruit.

Easy to, easy not to.

Questions:

- *We get good at the things we practice; if we practice the piano, we get good at it. Likewise, if we practice worrying, we get 'good' at worrying. What daily habits are you practising? What harvest is this producing?*

....

....

....

....

....

....

- *What seeds would you like to sow more often? What steps can you take to achieve this?*

....

....

....

....

....

....

....

- *What seeds would you like to stop sowing? What steps could you take that would make sowing the harmful, unproductive seeds less likely or harder to do?*

....

....

....

....

....

....

....

"Easy to, easy not to."
~ Jim Rohn ~

5. Mining for Truth

"The privilege of a lifetime is to become who you really are."
~ Joseph Campbell [1] ~

Mining for Truth

After searching, we find treasure; it is work and requires effort, but we can find it. We can find the roots of our thoughts and in finding them change them! While we can't change the thoughts of our younger self, for they exist in the past, we can uncover and examine them and choose alternative thoughts for our present self through examination.

The job is this: We must observe, reflect and consider the effects of our thoughts on ourself, on others, upon our life and our circumstance.

We must be honest and clear, linking cause and effect through patient investigation. In all of our daily comings and goings, we must seek to learn and obtain wisdom and knowledge of ourselves. This work, this mining for truth, is the activity that yields understanding, wisdom and power.

In this endeavour, we find the spiritual law that 'whoever seeks shall find' and 'the door will be opened to whoever knocks on it'. Yet don't miss the point. Mining is work. This is labour. But what work! You are discovering the resources for powerful transformation. You are finding treasure!

Consider

Carl Jung wrote that *"until we make the subconscious conscious it will forever rule us, and we will call it fate,"* [2] and what powerful advice this is! Many of our beliefs and assumptions about ourselves and the world sit within our subconscious, out with our awareness yet consistently and steadily framing our experiences and guiding our actions.

A few years ago, while studying Transactional Analysis, I became aware of a belief I had been holding in my subconscious, that being 'I get close, but I never make it!' As I reflected on this belief, I saw its effect on my life. I would start a project or venture and, on experiencing an unexpected obstacle, would often give up, silently saying to myself, 'I always get close, but never make it!'. I felt this was just my luck, perhaps even my fate. While others would succeed, I would only ever get close, never quite managing to get there.

However, as soon as this belief came into my consciousness, I saw it for what it was, a very limiting and disempowering story. Since then, I have worked hard to replace this limiting belief with a far more enabling one. This began simply by noticing when I was telling myself this limiting story and mindfully putting it down and look for other interpretations of events. I can still very much feel invited into this limiting story, but through practice, I can better notice and decline these invitations. Overall, I now see obstacles as **on** my way rather than **in** my way, challenges to be embraced and opportunities to learn and grow.

Discovering the stories told within our subconscious is work, but it is the most wonderful kind of work, for in it, there is freedom. After bringing my 'close by not quite' story into my awareness, I saw it for the limiting story it was and make changes!

Reflect on the following quote:

"Surely something wonderful is sheltered inside you. I say this with all confidence, because I happen to believe we are all walking repositories of buried treasure. I believe this is one of the oldest and most generous tricks the universe plays on us human beings, both for its own amusement and for ours: The universe buries strange jewels deep within us all, and then stands back to see if we can find them. The hunt to uncover those jewels — that's creative living. The courage to go on that hunt in the first place — that's what separates a mundane existence from a more enchanted one."
~ Elizabeth Gilbert [3] ~

Questions:

- Are there stories you tell about yourself that reduce your options or limit your agency? If so, what are they?

....

....

....

....

....

....

....

- What limiting beliefs and/or assumptions are contained within these stories?

....

....

....

....

....

....

....

- Looking at these stories, what valuable insight have you uncovered?

....
....
....
....
....
....
....

"We find treasure after searching..."

6. Tending the Garden

"Sow a thought and you reap an action;
sow an action and you reap a habit;
sow a habit and you reap a character;
sow a character and you reap a destiny."
~ Smiles, Samuel [1] ~

Tending the Garden

What can we liken our minds to? A garden.

Gardens may be intelligently cared for and developed or allowed to run wild. Yet, notice this. Whether the garden is tended by the most expert and skilled gardener or neglected and allowed to run wild – the garden will bring forth!

There is no way to avoid this law; we reap what we sow.

But I sowed no seed you might say, well, if no useful seeds are put into the garden, then the world will supply an abundance of useless weeds.

Which garden will you live with? Live within? Like the good gardener, will you tend the garden of your mind, weeding out all the wrong, useless and damaging thoughts and cultivating the good thoughts, right, useful and pure. By working in this way, we soon discover that we are the master, the gardener of our soul, the director of our life, the captain of our ship.

We discover within ourselves the laws of thought and learn, with ever-growing skill and insight, how our thoughts shape and produce our character, circumstances and destiny.

Consider

Nelson Mandela is an inspiring figure for many reasons, but what inspires me most is the deliberate way he cultivated his inner self throughout his life.

I heard a TedTalk [2] once where the speaker told a story about Mandela's perspective of his time in prison. When asked about his time in prison, he described it as an opportunity to form within himself that which he desired to see formed across his nation (forgiveness). He wasn't wasting time or passing time or allowing harmful seeds to take root; he was sowing seed.

This was a consistent theme for Mandela, indeed, when asked on a different occasion how he survived prison, he answered simply, *'I didn't survive, I prepared!'* [3].

Reflect

"Someday, in the years to come, you will be wrestling with the great temptation, or trembling under the great sorrow of your life. But the real struggle is here, now...Now it is being decided whether, in the day of your supreme sorrow or temptation, whether you shall miserably fail or gloriously conquer. Character cannot be made except by steady, long continued process."
~ Phillips Brooks [4] ~

What preparation could you begin now?

What seeds could you sow?

To help you answer this question, it might help to consider your own life as a garden: what do you require to flourish? What needs to be trimmed back? What needs to be planted? What nourishment is required?

....

....

....

....

....

....

Action:

Think about a vision for your future that inspires you. It could be a new way of being such as peace, or forgiveness. It could be a relationship or a job. Whatever it is, meditate on this inspiring future. Now, mindfully consider what seeds you could sow now that will prepare you for this future.

....

....

....

....

....

Note three specific actions you will perform today and this week.

....

....

....

....

....

....

....

Invictus

By William Ernest Henley [5]

Out of the night that covers me,
Black as the pit from pole to pole,
I thank whatever gods may be
For my unconquerable soul.

In the fell clutch of circumstance
I have not winced nor cried aloud.
Under the bludgeonings of chance
My head is bloody, but unbowed.

Beyond this place of wrath and tears
Looms but the Horror of the shade,
And yet the menace of the years
Finds and shall find me unafraid.

It matters not how strait the gate,
How charged with punishments the scroll
I am the master of my fate,
I am the captain of my soul.

7. Conversations with ourself

"The self is made, not given."

~ Barbara Myerhoff [1] ~

Conversations with ourself

Our thoughts and our character are linked.

Our character is shown through the various ways we interact with our environment and react to the circumstances we encounter. The actions of our character reveal the inner discussions we have with ourselves.

In this, our outward conditions will always be harmoniously related to our inner life. This does not mean that our circumstance at any given time indicates our entire character, but that those circumstances are intimately connected with some key belief that we hold or story that we tell.

When in pain, look first to your thoughts. If nothing is found at first – dig deeper!

Consider

We demonstrate the thought-seeds that we have been planting through our actions. Our behaviours demonstrate the conversations we have been having with ourselves.

An easy way to observe this is through behaviours we often call 'out-bursts'.

Consider an individual who unleashes a torrent of angry words at their partner for leaving a used cup by the sink rather than putting it in the dishwasher: *"Do you think I'm your slave? Do you think I have nothing better to do than tidy up after you?"*

What is the 'out-burst'? It is the overflow of the conversation that the individual has been having with themselves: *"Why is it that I am the only person who ever tidies up? They just treat me like their personal slave!"*

Thoughts are seeds and these 'thought-seeds' will bring forth. We are wise when we pay attention to the 'thought-seeds' that we sow.

Some have said that we are the average of the five people we spend the most time with. I would argue that we are also the average of the five thoughts we think most often. Stop for a moment and consider the care that a loving parent would take regarding the five people they would allow to surround and influence their child. Do we give the same care to the thoughts that fill our psychological space?

Think of it like this, if your thoughts were people would you let them into your house? If you wouldn't let them into your house, then you probably shouldn't let them into your head! But what should we do with the thoughts that present themselves to us? Learning to be selective about the thoughts we 'let in' is a start, and from here, we can converse with our thoughts. *'You can't come in!'*, while useful can produce tension in the mind as we resist our thoughts. Speaking to our thoughts in the following way allows us to filter our thoughts while limiting the internal tension: *'I know you are here because you think you have been helpful in the past, but I have new thoughts that are more positive for me so you can go now.'*

Action

Listen to your mental chatter and notice the 'thought-seeds' you are planting. As you observe your thoughts, be curious about them and their effects on you. You might find it helpful to pay attention to any 'outbursts' that you have, either in public or by yourself.

After observing your thoughts and their effects on your behaviour and well-being, identify 'thought-seeds' that produce unwanted consequences and replace them.

"If your thoughts were people, would you let them into your house?"

8. Why are we here?

"Nature magically suits a man to his fortunes, by making them the fruit of his character."
~ Ralph Waldo Emerson [1] ~

Why are we here?

Everyone is where they are by the law and consequence of their being. The thoughts built into their character have brought them to where they now stand. There is no chance about it. There is sowing and there is reaping. This is as true for those who feel 'out of harmony' with their surroundings as it is for those content with them.

Regardless of where we are, in comfort or in pain, we will learn and grow from our circumstances. We find that when we learn the lesson that is there for us, circumstances pass on and something new takes its place.

Consider

*"Everyone is where they are by...consequence of... the
thoughts which have been built into their character..."*

What does it mean to build character?

When I worked in primary schools, I told the children that
the only part of them that grew automatically was their
bodies; their emotions and minds only grew through
deliberate work. *"I don't want a seven-year-old walking
around in a twelve-year-old's body."* I would tell them.

The same is true for all of us. We might be forty years old in
our bodies but have the patience of a nine-year-old or the
temper of a toddler. Our bodies grow and develop naturally;
our emotions, or perhaps more accurately, the mastery of
our emotions, only comes through deliberate effort. In this
sense, our character will develop over time regardless of any
specific actions. However, developing a particular character
composed of particular qualities and deliberately chosen
and cultivated attributes requires work and attention.

What then is the forty-year-old to do, who discovers the
patience of a nine-year-old within them? They must lovingly
and patiently instruct this childlike part of themselves, so it
matures. They must treat this part of them as a child and
guide it, growing it until it makes up what has been lacking.

Actions

Observe yourself today and be curious about aspects that might benefit from further development. After some consideration, choose one area and think about how you could develop this part of yourself lovingly and encouragingly.

It might help to imagine this part of yourself as a child you are instructing: How would you speak to this child? What would your tone be like? How would you ensure the child didn't feel blame, shame or judgement as they learn and develop?

No one has ever thrived under feelings of blame, shame or guilt. When we notice underdeveloped parts of ourselves, we shouldn't engage these negative emotions.

"Character is, in the long run, the decisive factor in the life of individuals and of nations alike."
~ Theodore Roosevelt [2] ~

9. Strength in the Storm

*"Don't pray for better winds.
Pray for the wisdom to set a better sail!"*
~ Jim Rohn [1] ~

Strength in the Storm

We find ourselves buffeted by circumstance if we believe that we are at the whim of outside conditions. However, when we realise that we possess creative powers and may command the hidden soil and seed of our being, out of which circumstances grow, we become our own master and a slave to circumstance no more.

The truth is our circumstances grow out of our thoughts. For any length of time, whoever has practised self-control and self-purification will have noticed that the positive alteration in their circumstances has been in exaction proportion with their altered mental condition.

This might sound hard, yet anyone who has spent time earnestly applying themselves to remedy the defects in their character soon discovers this to be true. As our thoughts change, we find that our environment changes also.

Our souls attract what they secretly long for and love and also that which they fear. We find that our circumstances are how our souls receive their own whether reaching the heights of their aspirations or falling to the lowest level of despair or depravity.

Consider:

"The truth is our circumstances grow out of our thoughts."

Have you ever had the experience of buying a new car or piece of clothing and suddenly you notice it everywhere? The interesting thing about this phenomenon is that noticing these items was always possible; seeing them was always an option. Yet you didn't see them. Previously these items were not a part of your story, and, as such, your brain filtered them out as unneeded detail. However, now that these items are part of your story, your brain focuses on these details, and you see them.

Suppose for a moment that your story contains the expectation that people don't value you. Your brain will look for and bring forward the details which confirm this story. Yet consider the previous example of suddenly seeing a particular car everywhere you go. Seeing it was always an option, but you didn't until it became part of your story. Is it not equally possible that 'seeing' examples of people valuing you could also be possible if it were part of your story?

In very simple terms, we get what we look for.

Action

Read the following activity and then take a few moments to mindfully imagine what is being described.

Choose an emotion you would like to experience more of, for example, gratitude, love or peace. Now imagine programming your brain so it is extra-sensitive to instances that communicate these emotions such that it will now pull into focus what previously you might have missed.

As you engage in this practice, remember that you can also stop throughout your day and tune back into your chosen emotion.

Developing the habit of asking, *'What else is available? What else could I notice?'* is another strategy to support this practice.

"The mental construction of our daily activities, more than the activity itself, defines our reality."
~ Shawn Anchor [2] ~

10. Shaping our worlds

Part 1

"The fountain of content must spring up in the mind, and he who hath so little knowledge of human nature as to seek happiness by changing anything but his own disposition, will waste his life in fruitless efforts and multiply the grief he proposes to remove."
~ Samuel Johnson [1] ~

Shaping our worlds
Part 1

Every thought sown or allowed to fall into the mind and take root will produce its own. Sooner or later, these 'thought-seeds' will grow into action or word and become reality. As the 'thought-seeds' grow, they become the stories we tell ourselves and the lens through which we see and experience the world.

If we plant the 'thought-seed' that person X is against us, this seed will soon bloom and circumstance will soon allow us to experience person X in this way.

However, should we plant the 'thought-seed' that person X is for us, we will interpret all of their doing and being through this belief. Once again, we will find that circumstance will soon allow us to experience person X in this way.

We plant our 'thought-seeds', and we harvest their fruit.

Which harvest do you wish?

Good thoughts will bear good fruit, bad thoughts bad fruit.

Consider:

John and Sarah are ten years old and work at the same desk in their classroom. John comes back from sharpening his pencil and notices that his rubber is now on Sarah's side of the desk. In a sudden rush of anger, he yells to the teacher, 'Sarah just stole my rubber!'

On review, we see two things in this scenario; one is factual, the other fictional. John notices that his rubber is now on Sarah's side of the desk; this is factual. He then guesses why it is on Sarah's side of the desk; this is fictional. But which of the two causes John pain? The fact or the fiction? The notice or the guess?

John's pain didn't come from the facts, his rubber now being on Sarah's side of the desk, but from the meaning he gave to these facts, Sarah stole his rubber.

Like John, our pain is often caused by the meaning we give to events; we create fictional stories to describe what has happened. We notice something (factual) and then guess what it means (fictional), with our guesses being drawn from the story we tell about ourselves and the world.

The story that John tells is that everyone is out to get him, and as a result, he normally interprets events in this way. But John is only guessing, he is creating a fictional story to explain events and the story he is telling is hurting him.

So what is John to do? He should start by checking his guess as his guess is causing him pain; perhaps Sarah simply borrowed his rubber and forgot to put it back. With a new habit of checking his guesses, John can update his story; not everyone is out to get him.

Guessing doesn't just occur in classrooms; we notice and guess in our relationships and in our professional lives, and the consequences of a 'bad guess' can be far-reaching.

During my first week in a new promoted post, I walked to the kitchen to make my first coffee of the day. On my way, I was greeting my new colleagues with a friendly 'good morning' when I received – as I experienced it – a very cool response from one colleague. By the time I had arrived at the office kitchen, my stomach was in knots as I guessed what this cool response meant – 'She doesn't rate me', 'She thinks I'm too young for this post', 'She thinks I'm underqualified'. Luckily, I noticed my guess and considered what else her response might have meant, a bad start to her day, car problems on the way to work or preoccupation with a pressing matter. However, notice this, had I not checked my guess, there would have been very real consequences on an organisational level. The negative feelings produced by my guess would have made me less likely to approach this colleague for advice or support, less likely to include them in meetings or teams and most likely would have made me less likely to share well in meetings where they were present.

All of this from a guess!

Check your guess!

"Good thoughts will bear good fruit, bad thoughts bad fruit."

Action:

Over the coming days and weeks, try and notice when you are making a guess. You might find it helpful to voice your guess as you notice it, for example:

"I notice that I'm guessing his intention was..."

"I notice that I'm guessing this happened because..."

As you voice your guess, be curious about what other interpretations might be available.

Remember that you also may check your guess by asking questions. When checking your guess with another person, research professor Brene Brown recommends using the phrase *'The story that I'm telling myself is...'* as this creates space for, and indeed invites, the other person's story. For example:

"I notice that you were late for dinner and the story that I'm telling myself is that you don't value the time it takes me to prepare food for us."

"If I could give men and women in relationship and leaders and parents one hack, I would give them, 'the story I'm making up. *Basically, you're telling the other person your reading of the situation — and simultaneously admitting that you know it can't be 100% accurate."*
~ Brene Brown [2] ~

11. Shaping our Worlds

Part 2

"The paradox seems to be...that the truly free individual is free only to the extent of his own self-mastery. While those who will not govern themselves are condemned to find masters to govern over them."
~ Steven Pressfield [1] ~

Shaping our Worlds

Part 2

The outer world of circumstance shapes itself to the inner world of thought.

The laws of growth, sowing, and reaping are consistent and unchanging and as the reaper of our own harvest, we learn this truth both by suffering and bliss. The wise learn this truth and take responsibility, the foolish ignore it, blaming others instead for the circumstances in which they live.

Our lives do not develop by happenstance or chance but are the natural outworking of the thoughts we submit ourselves to, be these foul and unhealthy or strong and pure and when harvest time comes, we must all gather in the fruit of our thought life. We must live in the outer conditions we have created.

Rarely does one become bankrupt or imprisoned by the tyranny of fate or circumstance but by the pathway of grovelling thoughts and base desires. Neither does a pure-minded person fall suddenly into crime because of external forces. Rather that criminal thought which has now bloomed into action had been planted and secretly cared for in the heart. As it grew in the mind, it also grew in power, and its blooming became inevitable.

Be quite clear on this point: Circumstance does not make the man; it reveals him to himself!

We do not find ourselves continually in vice or suffering apart from cultivating vicious inclinations and thoughts. Likewise, we will not consistently ascend into virtue and its happiness without the ongoing cultivation of virtuous aspirations and ideas. As the sower of thought-seeds, man is the maker of himself and the shaper and author of his environment.

Consider:

We become what we practice.

If our habit is to practice anger, then we will become 'good' at being angry and our body will stand ready to produce anger. Our practice will make us so good at being angry that it will hardly take any effort at all to produce anger.

If our habit is to practice sadness, we will become 'good' at being sad, and our body will stand ready to produce sadness. Our practice will make us so good at being sad that it will hardly take any effort at all to produce sadness.

We become what we practise. What are you practising?

Actions

Practice is liberating as it creates a more enabling way to approach personal development. Changing a practice feels less daunting than changing who we are.

Over the next couple of days, consider:

We become what we practice.

- What feelings, thoughts and behaviours are you practising? This kind of practice can often be embedded within routines, for example, getting cross when driving or complaining about work with a particular colleague.

....

....

....

....

....

....

- What feelings, thoughts and/or behaviours would you like to practice more? Can you think of routines that you could embed this practice within, for example, thinking of things you are grateful for while brushing your teeth?

....

....

....

....

....

....

"Circumstance does not make the man, it reveals him to himself!"

12. Attracting what you are

*"He is greatest whose strength carries up the most
hearts by the attraction of his own."*
~ Henry Ward Beecher [1] ~

Attracting what you are

We do not attract what we want, but what we are. While we are not our thoughts, we do become them and so it is those thoughts we feed with the most regularity, through inner conversation and agreement, which come forth. Be it good or bad, it is the tended seed that grows best.

The 'divinity that shapes our ends' is in ourselves, it is our very self. In truth, man liberates or imprisons himself. The seed of thought he sows being the prison warden or the liberating angel.

Do not be naive about this; we do not get what we wish for, but what we justly earn. We reap what we sow. Our wishes and prayers are only answered when they harmonize with our thoughts and actions.

Consider:

Consider these quotes from the passage. What comes to mind as you reflect on them?

- *"We do not attract that which we want, but that which we are."*

....

....

....

....

....

....

- *"While we are not our thoughts, we do become them."*

....

....

....

....

....

....

- *"In truth man liberates or manacles himself. The thought-seed he sows being either the prison warden or the liberating angel."*

....

....

....

....

....

Actions

Identify three positive characteristics you are most drawn to in others. In the space below, deliberately create a plan to cultivate these characteristics over the coming weeks. This might be a list, mind map or any other format that works for you. Set a date in your diary now when you will review the progress you have made.

"What you think you become.
What you feel you attract.
What you imagine you create."

~ Dr Joseph Murphy [2] ~

13. Fighting Against Circumstance

"So much time and effort is spent on wanting to change, trying to change, to be somebody different, better, or new. Why not use this time to get comfortable with yourself as you are instead?"
~ Andy Puddicombe [1] ~

Fighting Against Circumstance

Take a moment and reflect on this, for it is the reality of what we have discussed. We might continually revolt and fight against the circumstances of life. However, these circumstances are an outward effect produced by what we have nourished and preserved.

We fight against the effect yet cause the growth within us.

The cause may be a conscious vice or an unconscious weakness, but whatever it may be, it will bring forth, and we, being wise, must do battle against the cause and not the effect. We must be clear-headed about this! If we are eager to improve our circumstances but neglect to improve ourselves, we will remain bound!

To move forward, something in you must change. Forward movement is won by those who do not shrink from pruning and weeding their inner worlds.

Consider:

Is it true or even helpful to say that circumstances are an outward effect produced from what we have nourished and preserved within? This idea could be harmful, taken to an extreme, implying that an individual's illness or other such tragedies are caused or produced by the individual. Used as an instrument of blame, this idea further compounds the individual's suffering by making it their fault. This is not the meaning of this text; rather, this is an invitation to look again and discover opportunity within the midst of challenge.

An appraisal is a judgement of value; houses, antiques and artistic and athletic performances can all undergo appraisal. Reappraisal is when we look again, reconsider and perhaps re-evaluate based on a new or more informed set of criteria. For example, I might look at an old painting and give it a fairly low appraisal, judging it solely against my artistic preferences. However, the same painting may benefit from the reappraisal of an art collector who, looking with a different set of criteria, may find the painting worth a great deal of money. The reappraisal changes the painting, my relationships to and thoughts and feelings about the painting and also presents new options – I could sell the painting and get rich or donate it to a museum for all to enjoy.

Cognitive reappraisal is when we 'look again' at situations we are facing and reappraise them, seeking to identify challenges and threats within them. This is not naïve optimism or an insensitive reduction of the challenges faced. Rather it is the deliberate decision to believe this situation may also include challenges from which I can.

Interestingly, research has yet to find a limit to the situations which can benefit from cognitive reappraisal. Here are a few examples of challenges in which cognitive reappraisal has produced a positive result:

- HIV and cancer patients reported lower rates of depression and anxiety when approaching their diagnosis as a challenge as well as a threat[2].

- Couples struggling to conceive reported happier relationships with fewer arguments when viewing the situation as a challenge[3].

- Setting specific challenges improved individuals' mental and physical health coping with the death of a spouse[4].

It appears then that when we face situations out with our control, looking inward and reappraising the situation can change our experience and change it for the better. In the studies listed above, the participants still had cancer, struggled to conceive a child, and still lost a spouse. Still, they reduced their suffering by turning inward, making inner changes, and even experiencing growth.

Actions

Adaptive Coping

An adaptive coping strategy changes either the situation or your experience. Cognitive reappraisal is an example of adaptive coping.

Learning to use Cognitive Reappraisal

Begin by reflecting on a difficult situation you experienced in the past. As you reflect on this situation, look to identify the benefits of this experience. For example:

- *I am wiser because of this experience.*

- *I have a greater appreciation for my health.*

- *I have learnt that I am stronger that I realise.*

- *I can be brave when I need to be.*

- *I made friendships which I treasure.*

- *I gained a greater understanding of my own values and priorities.*

....

....

....

....

....

....

Now consider a challenge you are facing; what benefits might be nested within? Make a list:

....

....

....

....

....

....

Adaptive Coping and Transformative Communication

Transformative communication is another adaptive coping response. Transformative communication simply means paying attention to and making deliberate choices about our language to communicate events to ourselves. For example, when you find yourself stuck in traffic, you can choose to say, "What a nightmare!" or "I can use this as a moment to slow down."

Thinking about the situation you are facing and the benefits you have identified as potentially existing within it, list some sentences you will deliberately make use of.

Here is an example.

I have an upcoming assignment assessed via a 10-minute presentation. Faced with this situation, I could spiral into negative self-talk – *"This is a nightmare! I'll never manage! This makes me so nervous and stressed! I can't speak in front of people!"* We would soon identify the presentation as a threat to be avoided.

Using cognitive reappraisal and transformative communication we could do the following:

Cognitive Reappraisal:

- *"Ok, I'm feeling nervous about giving this presentation, but this is an opportunity to develop my communication skills which will be really useful for me in my career and in my social life. Facing this challenge will make me feel proud and it's a great opportunity to develop my inner strength."*

Transformative Communication:

I will choose to tell myself the following:

- *"It's ok to be a learner at this, I've learnt to do lots of things in the past."*

- *"This is a great opportunity to grow in ways that are meaningful to me."*

- *"I'll be proud that I faced this challenge."*

- *"This is tough, but it's helping me grow."*

Now it's your turn:

Cognitive reappraisal:

....

....

....

....

....

....

Transformative Communication

- I will choose to tell myself:

....

....

....

....

....

....

"So much time and effort is spent on wanting to change, trying to change, to be somebody different, better, or new. Why not use this time to get comfortable with yourself as you are instead?"

~ Andy Puddicombe [1] ~

14. The Cause of the Effect

"Man is not the creature of circumstances;
circumstances are the creatures of men.
We are free agents, and man is more powerful than
matter."
~ Benjamin Disraeli [1] ~

The Cause of the Effect

Consider these three cases:

The Poor Man

This man hates his poverty and longs to see his surroundings and home comforts improved, yet he always looks for ways to avoid his work and cut corners. This avoidance finds its root in the belief he is entitled to deceive and cheat his employer due to the low wages he receives.

This man demonstrates his complete lack of understanding of the principles that are the basis of prosperity but, more damagingly, is actively attracting deeper poverty by dwelling in and acting out lazy, deceptive and weak thoughts. He shows himself to be unfitted to rise out of his wretchedness through his thoughts and actions.

The Rich Woman

The rich woman suffers from a painful and persistent disease due to her gluttony. She is willing to pay large sums of money to get rid of the disease and its painful symptoms, yet will not put a stop to her gluttonous desires. She wants to indulge her desire for food and have her health as well. Such a woman is unfit to have health because she has not yet learnt the first principles of a healthy life.

The Crooked Employer

This employer uses crooked means to avoid paying his employees a fair wage, hoping to make a larger profit for himself. Such an employer is unfit for prosperity, yet when he finds himself bankrupt, both regarding his riches and his reputation, he blames circumstance. He cannot see he is the sole author of his condition.

The Cause of the Effect

These three examples illustrate the truth that we cause our circumstances, though this is nearly always at an unconscious level.

While we may aim at a good and worthy end, our inner disposition may be such that through our conduct we continually sabotage our successes by indulging thoughts and desires which cannot possibly harmonize with or bring about the end we seek.

Good thoughts and actions can never produce bad results; bad thoughts and actions can never produce good results.

Consider:

Stephen Covey, the author of 'The Seven Habits of Highly Successful People', tells the story of a nurse who interrupted one of his seminars. For years this nurse had cared for, in her words, an ungrateful misery of a man who constantly found fault with her, criticised her and never once gave a word of thanks. In her mind, this man had made her life a misery. Yet, as she listened to Covey teach about Habit 1: Be Proactive, she became angrier.

Covey taught that between every stimulus, there is a space where we have the freedom to choose our response and that ultimately, no one can hurt us without our consent. In this way, proactive people are not a victim to circumstances but embrace their ability to choose their response to the situations they encounter. Where proactive people act, reactive people are acted upon.

As the nurse listened, she became enraged at the suggestion that somehow her experience could have been different had she made different choices. Surely this misery of a man was responsible for the poor quality of life she had experienced over the last few years. Yet, as she sat in the auditorium, she considered Covey's words, turning them over in her mind, "Do I have the power to choose my response?"

"When I finally realised that I do have that power, when I swallowed that bitter pill and realised that I had chosen to be miserable, I also realised that I could choose not to be miserable. At that moment I stood up. I felt as though I was let out of San Quentin. I wanted to yell to the whole

world, 'I am free! I am let out of prison! No longer am I going to be controlled by the treatment of some person.'"[2]

Reflect

Reactive thinking places the problem and the solution 'out there', which gives away its power to change.

Proactive thinking takes responsibility for the problem and the solution and also takes possession of the power to change!

Actions

- What situation or relationship would you like to change?

....

....

....

....

....

....

- In what ways have you co-created this situation/relationship?

....

....

....

....

....

....

- What can you do to improve your response to this situation or relationship?

....

....

....

....

....

....

"Every time you think the problem is 'out there,'
that very thought is the problem."
~ Stephen Covey [2] ~

15. Learning from Adversity

*"Criticism may not be agreeable, but it is necessary.
It fulfils the same function as pain in the human body. It
calls attention to an unhealthy state of things."*
~ Winston Churchill [1] ~

Learning from Adversity

A person's inner condition cannot be known solely by reflecting on their circumstance. A person may be honest in certain aspects of their life and yet suffer lack. Another may be dishonest in certain areas and yet acquire wealth. It is superficial judgement which assumes that a dishonest person is almost totally corrupt or that an honest person is almost entirely virtuous. The dishonest person may have admirable virtues which the good person does not possess, and the honest person likely has certain obnoxious vices absent in the other.

The honest person reaps the results of their honest thoughts and actions and equally reaps the suffering their vices produce. Likewise, the dishonest person lives with their own suffering and happiness.

It is a pleasing story to tell that we suffer from our virtues, yet not until we have removed every selfish, bitter and impure thought from our minds can we be in a position to know that our sufferings result from our good and not our bad qualities. Rather than to assume that we suffer because of our virtues, it is advisable to assume that the Great Law of reaping and sowing is at work. This law is absolutely just and cannot give good for evil or evil for good.

When we acknowledge the law of reaping and sowing, we empower ourselves to change.

Consider:

The famous Christian evangelist Billy Graham would, occasionally, meet with reporters and journalists who had publicly criticised him[2]. When asked about this, he replied that he felt it a good practice to turn his critics into coaches. While there is wisdom in not allowing every person you meet to speak into your life, there is also folly in thinking that no one sees situations clearly besides you! The practice of turning critics into coaches embraces the truth that sometimes, the challenges we face are of our own making.

It's helpful to reframe problems as questions we don't yet have an answer for. However, notice these problems become issues when we add judgement. An effective strategy for dealing with issues or problems is tracing them back to the unanswered question by stripping away any judgement and leaving the clean information.

When we turn critics into coaches and consider the extent to which the challenges we face are of our own making, we are gaining access to new and possibly unconsidered information, which may well answer the question we have struggled with.

Feedback doesn't have to include blame, shame or judgement.

It can just be information.

Actions

Think of a problem or issues you have faced or are facing. Strip away any judgement that surrounds this issue until you arrive at your unanswered question. Now that you see the question clearly, what answers do you have?

....

....

....

....

....

Think of a situation when you were criticised. Remove any judgement that may have been attached to the feedback and consider the 'clean' information. How can you use this 'clean' information to move forward?

....

....

....

....

....

"The trouble with most of us is that we'd rather be ruined by praise than saved by criticism."
~ Norman Vincent Peale [3] ~

"Let me never fall into the vulgar mistake of dreaming that I am persecuted whenever I am contradicted."
~ Ralph Waldo Emerson [4] ~

16. Corn from Corn & Nettles from Nettles

"Success leaves clues,
and if you sow the same seeds,
you'll reap the same rewards."
~ Brad Thor [1] ~

Corn from Corn & Nettles from Nettles

Good thoughts and actions can never produce bad results; bad thoughts and actions can never produce good results.

This is another way of saying that nothing can come from corn but corn, nothing from nettles but nettles.

In the natural world, we understand this law and work with it, but we can struggle to understand and co-operate with this law in the mental and moral world even thoughts its operation here is as simple and undeviating.

Consider:

Reflect on these quotes:

> *"We are what we repeatedly do.*
> *Excellence, then, is not an act, but a habit."*
> ~ Will Durant [2] ~

Actions:

Choose an individual who inspires you and undertake some research about this person seeking to identify the daily habits and practices that have helped them to achieve the results you admire.

This could be a couple whose relationship you admire, a friend whose character inspires you or star performer in a field that interests you.

- What seeds do they sow to produce this harvest?

....

....

....

....

....

....

- What specific actions do they take?

....

....

....

....

....

....

- What specific beliefs do they hold?

....

....

....

....

....

....

*"We are what we repeatedly do.
Excellence, then, is not an act, but a habit."*
~ Will Durant ~

17. Suffering

"I am an old man and have known a great many troubles, but most of them never happened."
~ Mark Twain [1] ~

Suffering

Wrong thinking always produces suffering and suffering of this nature indicates that the individual is out of harmony with themselves and with the law of sowing and reaping. Yet this suffering has a purpose, it is to instruct, to purify and to burn out all that is useless and impure – if we will learn from it!

The contrast to this state of suffering is blessedness, which results from mental harmony. This is an important lesson, blessedness, not material possessions, is the measure of right thinking and wretchedness, not lack of material possessions, is the measure of wrong thinking. A man may be utterly miserable yet rich or completely at peace, full of joy and poor.

Blessedness and riches are only joined when the riches are rightly and wisely used.

Poverty and indulgence are the two extremes of wretchedness and are both equally unnatural and the result of mental disorder. A person is not rightly conditioned until they are a happy, healthy and prosperous being and happiness, health and prosperity result from a harmonious adjustment of the inner with the outer, of the individual with their surroundings.

Consider:

How would you define 'quality of life'? It's easy to quickly think of elements such as money, position and possessions, but when we think a little slower, it is also easy to think of people who have 'had it all' and yet still been miserable and, ultimately, experienced a very low quality of life.

Your quality of life is the total of all the emotions you feel in a day. Have you spent all of today feeling frustrated and rushed? Well, that's your quality of life for today!

The quality of our lives is the total of the emotions we experience, so we should strive, whenever possible, for positive experiences.

There is a wonderful movie called 'About Time'[2] in which the main character can travel through time. Towards the end of the movie, this character decides to stop time travelling and live solely in the present. To prepare himself for this transition, he lives every day twice, doing this so he can spot the points in his day when he was worrying or becoming angry or frustrated when actually, things turned out fine. Then, on his second go through the same day, he doesn't worry that he'll miss his bus or become frustrated with his children or snap at a co-worker; he knows it will be ok. He does this until one day he realises that he no longer needs to live the day again, he can simply choose not to worry or become frustrated the first time through.

Actions:
At the end of the day, consider what the total of all your emotional experiences has been. What quality of life did this produce?

....

....

....

....

....

If you got to relive today again, what would you do differently?

....

....

....

....

....

"The most important trick to be(ing) happy is to realize that happiness is a choice that you make and a skill that you develop. You choose to be happy, and then you work at it. It's just like building muscles."
~ Naval Ravikant [3] ~

18. Accepting the Hidden Justice

"The same wind blows on us all. What makes the difference between where we are one week, one month, one year from now is not the blowing of the wind but the setting of the sail."
~ Jim Rohn [1] ~

Accepting the Hidden Justice

We become the best version of ourselves when we stop complaining and look for the hidden justice which regulates our lives. Once found, we must accept this hidden justice and work with it, adapting our minds to its truth.

We do this first by taking responsibility for ourselves, no longer blaming others as the cause of our condition but instead building ourselves up through strong and noble thoughts.

Rather than kicking against circumstance, we seek to use them as aids to more rapid progress and to discover the hidden powers and possibilities within ourselves.

Consider:

Steven Covey explores the above ideas through a model he calls 'circles of influence and concern'[2]. The simple yet powerful idea is that we should move situations out of our circle of concern and into our circle of influence. The challenge is this move requires us to take responsibility for the situation. However, in taking responsibility for it, we also gain power to influence and change it. Consider the following example:

As a university lecturer, I often observe student teachers as part of their teaching placements, and it is common for them to say, "I hope you pass me!" This is a perfect example of 'circle of concern' thinking.

When thinking this way, the student has given away all their influence and power, it is up to the tutor whether or not they pass. However, in giving away power, they can feel free of responsibility, after all, it's up to the tutor whether or not they pass! This is the lure of 'circle of concern' thinking; it lets you off the hook! If the student fails, they can blame the tutor or anything else!

'Circle of Influence' thinking would say something like *It's up to me to demonstrate to my tutor that I meet these criteria. It's up to me whether or not I pass!* Notice that this kind of thinking has taken responsibility for the situation and can influence it.

Taking responsibility for a situation differs from saying the situation is your fault. If a student has a particularly tricky class or unsupportive teacher, this isn't their fault, but by moving the situation into their circle of influence, they gain power to change it.

Responsibility differs from fault or blame.

Actions:

- What 'hidden justice' might be at work in your life? What lesson could it be teaching you?

....

....

....

....

....

- What situation can you move from your circle of concern into your circle of influence? How will you do this?

....

....

....

....

....

"Most people find the meaning in their life through responsibility."
~ Jordan Peterson [3] ~

19. The Law of the Universe

"What we choose to focus on and what we choose to ignore defines the quality of our life."
~ Cal Newport [1] ~

The Law of the Universe

Law, not confusion, is the dominating principle in the universe. Justice, not injustice, is the soul and substance of life and righteousness, not corruption, is the moulding and moving force in the spiritual government of the world.

The proof of this truth is in every person, set some time aside for honest and systematic introspection and self-analysis and you will find this to be true. We reap what we sow.

Consider this, by radically altering their thoughts, a person can effect rapid transformation. We imagine that our thoughts can be kept secret, but they cannot. Our thoughts rapidly crystallize into habit and habit brings forth circumstance.

Poor thoughts, be they mean, impure, fearful, weak, lazy, selfish, dishonest or hateful crystallize into destructive habits which solidify into conditions of poverty, poor health, emotional distress, adverse circumstance, failure, isolation and persecution.

But beautiful thoughts of all kinds crystallise into habits of grace, kindness, self-control, courage, productivity, gentleness, selflessness and self-reliance, which solidify into conditions of positive circumstance, peace, joy, success, plenty, freedom, protective and preservative circumstance, prosperity and true riches.

Any thought we continue to nurture and turn over in our mind, be it good or bad, cannot fail to produce its results on our character and circumstance. We cannot directly choose our circumstance, but we can all choose our thoughts, and so indirectly, yet surely, shape our circumstances.

Consider:

Reflect on these quotes:

> *"What you focus on is what you feel."*
> ~ Tony Robbins [2] ~

> *"My experience is what I agree to attend to."*
> ~ William James [3] ~

Actions:

- What thoughts do you nurture and return to most often?

....

....

....

....

....

....

- What do you focus your attention on?

  Consider:

  - positive/negative

  - threat/challenge

  - problem/opportunity

  - criticism/feedback

....

....

....

....

....

....

- How might these 'thought habits' be affecting you?

....

....

....

....

....

....

- How might these 'though habits' be shaping your circumstances?

....

....

....

....

....

....

"We cannot directly choose our circumstance, but we can all choose our thoughts, and so indirectly, yet surely, shape our circumstance."

20. Thoughts Make a Way

*"The happiness of your life
depends upon the quality of your thoughts."*
~ Marcus Aurelius [1] ~

Thoughts Make a Way

The law of sowing and reaping helps us all to the gratification of our thoughts. As we cultivate a particular thought, we will find that opportunities are presented to transform the thought into deed. Whether the seed is good or bad, the harvest will come.

When we stop harmful thoughts, we will soon find that all the world will soften towards us, not only that, but be ready to help us! When we put away poor and shameful thoughts, we will find that opportunities will spring up to aid us in our new resolve.

Consider this, the world is your kaleidoscope and the varying combinations of colours, which at every succeeding moment it presents to you are the exquisitely adjusted pictures of your ever-moving thoughts.

Consider:
Tony Robbins grew up in poverty with an abusive father. One day there was a knock on the door and Tony, then a child, opened the door to find a stranger waiting with a food parcel. Tony's father had also heard the knock on the door and was soon standing behind Tony, glaring at the man with the food parcel.

"Do you think I'm some kind of charity case?" Tony's father demanded angrily, *"Do you think I can't provide for my family?!"* and with this went to slam the door in the stranger's face. However, the stranger was not to be turned away this easily. Blocking the door with his foot, he looked Tony's dad in the eye and responded, *"Sir, don't let your family suffer for your pride."* Saying this, he handed the food parcel to Tony's father and left.

This event changed the lives of both Tony and his father. Tony went on to, amongst other ventures, start a charity that provides food parcels for millions of people each year. Tony's father left his family the next day. Tony believes the reasons for the two reactions was the asking and answering of the three following questions:

- *What will I focus on?*
- *What does this mean?*
- *What will I do next?*

Tony's father focused on a stranger thinking his family needed help. The meaning he gave to this was that he was a failure as a father and a man, what he did next was leave!

Tony focused on the fact that strangers care and will help. For him, this meant that he, too, could be a stranger that would care and offer help. What did he do next? Through partnering with the charity Feed American[2] Tony has helped the organisation feed 46.5 million people in the US each year. That is the equivalent of 1 in 7 Americans!

Actions

Reflect on a recent event and answer these questions:

- *Why did I focus on?*

....

....

....

....

....

- *What meaning did I give to the event?*

....

....

....

....

....

- *What did I do based on this?*

....

....

....

....

....

Now consider:
- *What else could you have focused on?*

....

....

....

....

....

- *What other meaning could you have given to the event?*

....

....

....

....

....

- *What else could you have done in response?*

....

....

....

....

....

....

"...the world is your kaleidoscope and the varying combinations of colours, which at every succeeding moment it presents to you are the exquisitely adjusted pictures of your ever-moving thoughts."

21. The Effect of Thought on Health & the Body

*"A person who has good thoughts cannot ever be ugly.
You can have a wonky nose and a crooked mouth and a
double chin and stick-out teeth, but if you have good
thoughts it will shine out of your face like sunbeams and
you will always look lovely."*
~ Roald Dahl [1] ~

The Effect of Thought on Health
& the Body

The body is the servant of the mind. Pause and think about this for a moment.

The body obeys the mind's instructions, whether deliberately given or the product of subconscious expression. Harmful thoughts will surely harm the body, causing all kinds of physical ailments. Yet healthy thoughts act as a tonic for the body, fortifying it with health and strength. Do not miss this point, disease and health, like circumstance, are related to our thoughts.

Sickly thoughts will express themselves through a sickly body. Negative and harmful thoughts can kill just as surely, though less rapidly, as a bullet. We only have to look around to see this is true. Anxiety and depression quickly demoralise the whole body and lay it open to the entrance of disease. Impure thoughts, even if not physically indulged, will soon shatter the nervous system.

The body is a delicate instrument that responds readily to the thoughts impressed upon it and these habits of thought will produce their own effects, be they good or bad. Thought is the source of action and of life; make the source pure and all will be pure.

If you would protect your body, guard your mind! If you would renew your body, beautiful your mind.

Consider:

In the Oscar Wilde novel 'The Portrait of Dorian Gray'[2], the main character remains permanently young and handsome despite his vile behaviour. However, while his physical body is unmarred by his actions, his portrait, housed safely in the attic, slowly changes to show on the outside what he has become on the inside.

Symmetry of our outer appearance mirroring our inner countenance is familiar. Consider these two quotes which describe this truth from opposite ends:

> *"Sin is a thing that writes itself across a man's face.*
> *It cannot be concealed."*
> ~ Oscar Wilde [2] ~

> *"A person who has good thoughts cannot ever be ugly.*
> *You can have a wonky nose and a crooked mouth and a*
> *double chin and stick-out teeth, but if you have good*
> *thoughts it will shine out of your face like sunbeams and*
> *you will always look lovely."*
> ~ Roald Dahl ~

Interestingly growing medical evidence speaks to a far deeper mirroring of our inner and outer states. Atherosclerosis is a cardiovascular disease caused by a buildup of plaque within the arteries of the heart. Over time the plaque hardens and produces a 'hard heart'.

It is well documented this hardening develops fastest in patients with high levels of pro-inflammatory chemicals in their bodies. In one study, researchers[3] investigated the link between negative emotions and atherosclerosis and discovered that the region of the brain responsible for regulating emotions also regulates the body's inflammatory response.

These findings suggest those individuals who engage in more negative thinking and experience more negative emotions appear to increase their risk of heart disease. Or, to use more poetic language, those individuals who cultivate negative and critical thinking habits in a real way develop hard hearts!

Actions

- Today, notice the link between your mind and your body. Pay attention to how certain thoughts affect your physical state.

....

....

....

....

....

....

- We can spend a great deal of time and care on our diet, mindfully choosing the food we consume. Today, reflect on the quality of your mental diet. What thoughts, ideas and beliefs are you feeding yourself? If someone else consumed your mental diet, how might it affect them?

....

....

....

....

....

....

- What simple steps could you take to improve your mental diet?

....

....

....

....

....

"We do not need to let our histories or our losses define us except in the way we choose. We can use them as fuel to create real depth, beauty, connectedness, and compassion in our lives. Our stories can make us exceptional people, not damaged ones. If we choose to be truthful with ourselves. And if we choose to digest and release the pain rather than try to avoid it. This is how pain accumulates and creates more pain, leading to neurosis, pathology, and brittleness of spirit."

~ Jewel [4] ~

22. Clean Thoughts/Clean Habits

"Socrates demonstrated long ago, that the truly free individual is free only to the extent of his own self-mastery."
~ Steven Pressfield [1] ~

Clean Thoughts/Clean Habits

A change of diet or routine does not change a person's thoughts. It is when we purify our thoughts we will no longer tend towards the damage we seek to remove.

Clean thoughts make clean habits!

Consider:

A couple of years ago, I noticed I had gained weight, so I used this as an opportunity to review my eating habits and make changes as I sought to lose the extra weight. After some research, I worked out how many calories my body needed each day; it was a lot less than I had been eating.

With this information, I followed my new eating plan and a strange thing happened, my stomach didn't agree with my plan! Throughout the day, I would feel hungry, despite my mind knowing I was eating enough calories and getting these calories through the right foods, my body would still send me a hungry message.

At this point, I had a choice, either believe the hungry message from my stomach or the nutritional information from my brain. As I considered this choice, I realized that my stomach had sent me hungry messages even when I was eating a lot more food. I guessed that even morbidly obese people probably still got hungry messages from their stomachs.

I realized that I needed to do more than change my eating habits if I wanted to eat healthily. I also needed to change my thinking. Improving my health required better quality thoughts as well as better quality foods!

Actions:

Reflect on the following quote:

"If our feelings control our actions, it is because we have abdicated our responsibility and empowered them to do so."

~ Steven Covey [2] ~

Can you think of a time when you 'abdicated responsibility'? How might clean thoughts have helped you?

....

....

....

....

....

....

Can you recognize a particular thought that sabotages your better intentions? It could be something as simple as *'That's too much work.'* or *'I never see things through.'*

....

....

....

....

....

....

If you were to 'clean up your thinking', what might this look like?

....

....

....

....

....

....

"You will never have a greater or lesser dominion than that over yourself...the height of a man's success is gauged by his self-mastery; the depth of his failure by his self-abandonment."
~ Leonardo da Vinci [3] ~

23. Protect your body by guarding your mind

"The story I'm telling myself is..."
~ Brené Brown [1] ~

Protect your body
by guarding your mind

There is no medicine as powerful in dissipating the body's ills as bright, cheerful thoughts. To live continually in thoughts of ill will, cynicism, suspicion and envy is to be confined in a self-made prison. But to think well of all, to be cheerful with all and to patiently learn to find the good in all, such unselfish thoughts as these are doors to heaven.

Dwelling day by day in thoughts of peace towards every person and every circumstance will bring abounding peace.

Consider:

In what ways can guarding our mind protect our body? Consider a time you received bad news, how did receiving this news affect you physically? Did you lose your appetite or even feel sick? What effect did the news have on your energy levels or your ability to focus? Mental events produce real changes in our bodies.

Consider:

Brené Brown, New York Times best-selling author, tells the story of a time she and her husband went for a swim in the lake[1], something they loved to do together. During the swim, she stopped to tell her husband how special he was to her and how much she enjoyed their time together, but instead of an equally romantic response, her husband gave only a short, vague reply. Brené felt hurt by his response but supposed that he may not have heard her, so tried again, stopping him again to tell him how much she loved him and appreciated this special time together. But once again, he only offered her a very brief response. This was not what Brene had anticipated and, understandably, she was hurt and upset.

Reflect for a moment on the physical symptoms that often accompany experiences such as these. To begin with, Brené was feeling happy, joyful and in love. Physiologically, happiness and joy are often accompanied by feelings of lightness, openness and presence. However, in response to the interactions with her husband, her feelings changed from happiness and love to hurt and anger, emotions often physically experienced through symptoms such as a churning stomach, headache and losing energy. This simple example clearly demonstrates how mental events produce real physical consequences. However, this is not the end of the story.

Rallying herself, Brené used a technique that her research had identified as the most consistent trait shared by resilient individuals. She shared her interpretation of the event and in doing so, created a space where inaccuracies could be addressed. Instead of believing her interpretation of the event (her husband was being distant and hurtful) and then living out the resulting feelings, she shared her experience using the phrase *'the story I'm telling myself is...'*

When she shared her 'story' with her husband, it turned out that he wasn't being dismissive but struggling with a panic attack. By checking the accuracy of her 'story', Brené avoided living out unwanted and damaging emotions.

Opening up our 'stories' allows us to calibrate how accurately we interpret events around us. This process of interpretation can also be thought of in terms of your 'explanatory style', that is, the style in which you tend to explain events to yourself. As you share the stories you are telling yourself, you will discern your explanatory style and address this. Remember, an inaccurate explanatory style, one out of touch with reality, produces unwanted emotional, mental and physical results.

Calibrating your explanatory style is an excellent example of how we can protect our bodies by guarding our minds.

Actions:

Over the coming days and weeks, make it a deliberate practice to voice the story you are telling yourself.

If sharing your 'story' with other people is too big a step, start by noticing the story you are telling and voicing it to yourself. As you become more confident and comfortable with this practice, share your 'story' with others.

As you engage in this practice, be curious about the explanatory style you discover. For example, you might ask questions such as:

- *What do I notice about my explanatory style?*

- *How accurate is it?*

- *In what ways is it helping me?*

- *In what ways is it getting in my way?*

- *What new information am I discovering?*

- *What can I do with this new information?*

- *What modifications might I make to my explanatory style?*

"Vulnerability sounds like truth and feels like courage. Truth and courage aren't always comfortable, but they're never weakness."
~ Brené Brown [2] ~

24. Aimlessness is a Vice

"Being busy is a form of laziness, lazy thinking and indiscriminate action."
~ Tim Ferris [1] ~

Aimlessness is a Vice

Until thought is linked with purpose, there is no intelligent accomplishment. Many people simply 'drift' through the ocean of life, yet this aimlessness is a vice! Such aimless drifting must not continue for the person who would steer clear of catastrophe and into achievement and success.

Those who have no central purpose in their life, no aim, fall as easy prey to petty worries, fears, troubles and self-pitying thoughts, which are indications of weakness and will lead to failure, unhappiness and loss just as surely, though by different routes, as deliberately planned sins.

Consider:

The Greek word *areté* means excellence or goodness, especially with function, so for instance, the *areté* of an ear is to hear, the *areté* of a car is to provide transportation, but what is the *areté* of a human? What is the excellence we should aim at? On one level of analysis there is no single target towards which all of humanity can be aimed. We can't all be hairdressers or firemen or famous sports stars, nor would we all want to be. Yet on another level of analysis we all share the common feature of being beings who aim at things and, when aiming correctly, find deep meaning and joy in pursuing the target towards which we strive.

The hero's journey [2] is a prime example of the power of aiming correctly. In each heroic story, the need is different, to restore balance in the force, to replace a stolen artefact, to destroy the ring of power. Yet, in some profound way, each story requires the same thing, a hero! And a hero aims correctly and accomplishes the required feat.

Interestingly the word 'sin' was originally a Greek archery term meant 'to miss the mark'. Sinning then is not simply 'doing bad things' but aiming at the wrong thing. It is easy to think of examples of people who have been damaged through pursuing the wrong thing, from making the wrong thing their aim in life. Aiming at the wrong thing can pull you apart. So, if aimlessness is a vice and aiming at the wrong thing is a 'sin' what should you be aiming at?

Aim at getting better at aiming!

Think about looking down a microscope or a pair of binoculars. At first, this is hard to do, and it takes time and practice to develop the skill. In the same way, "aiming" is itself a skill to be developed. Look around you today; what could you aim at? As you look seriously and curiously around you, targets will appear tidying up that mess, calling that family member, going for that walk at lunchtime, apologising for the thing you now regret doing (or not doing!). Choose one thing to aim at today and carefully and intentionally work to 'hit the target', to achieve the feat.

As you develop your 'aiming' abilities, you will see more targets and, importantly, develop the inner poise to aim at and hit these targets!

Actions:

Develop your aiming abilities!

We all have an innate talent for aiming, it is part of what makes us human. However, like any talent, it can be under practiced and underdeveloped. However, also like any talent, through effort, we can improve and develop.

To develop your aiming abilities, set yourself goals to aim at, begin small and allow yourself to be a beginner. Admiral William McRaven is famous for suggesting that we all begin each day by making our beds[3],

> *"If you make your bed every morning, you will have accomplished the first task of the day. It will give you a small sense of pride, and it will encourage you to do another task, and another, and another. And by the end of the day that one task completed will have turned into many tasks completed."*

"Routine in an intelligent man is a sign of ambition."
~ W.H. Auden [4] ~

"A life best lived is a life by design. Not by accident, and not by just walking through the day careening from wall to wall and managing to survive. That's okay. But if you can start giving your life dimensions and design and colour and objectives and purpose, the results can be staggering."
~ Jim Rohn [5] ~

25. Royal Road to Self-Control

"Would you have a great empire?
Rule over yourself."
~ Publius Syrus [1] ~

The Royal Road to Self-Control

We should hold within us a legitimate purpose, whether this is a spiritual ideal or worldly object, and then set out to accomplish it. Steadily focusing our thoughts on the object, we should make this purpose our supreme duty and devote ourselves to its attainment, not allowing our thoughts to wander in daydreams or longings. This is the royal road to self-control and true concentration of thought.

Even if we fail again and again to accomplish our purpose (which we must, until weakness is overcome and strength built). The strength of character gained is the true measure of our success and will form the starting point for future power and triumph.

For those who don't yet have a specific end in mind, they should fix their thoughts upon the faultless performance of their duties, no matter how insignificant the tasks may appear. Only in this way can our thoughts be gathered and focussed, and resolutions and energy developed.

The weakest soul, knowing its own weakness and believing the truth that strength can be developed only by effort and practice, will at once exert itself, and, adding effort to effort, patience to patience and strength to strength will never cease to develop and will, at last, grow strong!

Be sure of this, as the physically weak person can make themself strong by careful and patient training, so the person of weak thoughts can make themself strong by exercise in right thinking!

Consider:

Neuroplasticity refers to the brain's ability to form new pathways and to forget or lose old and/or underused pathways. At a very simple level, neuroplasticity suggests that the brain can be thought of as a field of grass, and as we learn, we walk new pathways across this field and the more we travel these pathways (through practice), the more established they become and the easier it is to travel them.

This picture of neuroplasticity is helpful when considering developing right thinking for several reasons. Firstly, it explains why new undertakings are hard – we haven't established a pathway yet! We are still blazing a trail through the field of grass; the journey still requires effort. This is important and worth noticing because it means that the difficulty we experience doesn't mean we aren't able or this new undertaking isn't really 'us'. It just means we haven't established a path yet! The second point to consider is that, just like a field of grass, if you stop using a path, the grass will grow back. This truth is perfectly summed up in the adage 'use it or lose it'!

Exercising right-thinking requires us to pay attention to these aspects of neuroplasticity as the thinking we habitually engage in becomes the well-worn paths we travel most easily. In this sense, we become what we practice. Equally, as we begin to reflect on the kind of thinking that might better serve us, we should anticipate these new patterns of thinking to be initially harder to travel due to their being less familiar and established and consequently requiring greater initial effort and practice.

Lastly, exercising right-thinking takes place on both a micro and a macro level. On the micro level, we set specific goals and work to attain them, for example, developing the mental habit of gratitude. On the macro level, we work to develop the inner strength required to be the kind of person who achieves goals.

While on the micro level, we will not achieve every goal we set, on a macro level, the pursuit of these goals is the kind of exercise that develops the inner strength required to achieve goals. The same can be said of exercise, which contains micro-goals of specific workouts (I will run 3 miles without stopping) nested within the macro goal of developing fitness. You may or may not achieve your micro goal of running 3 miles, but its attempt develops within you the inner strength to achieve goals of this nature. So too with right thinking.

Reflect:

Consider these two quotes:

*"We don't rise to the level of our expectations,
we fall to the level of our training."*
~ Archilochus [2] ~

*"Most people have the will to win,
few have the will to prepare to win."*
~ Bobby Knight [3] ~

Actions:

Reflect on these questions, writing down your answers:

- *What habits, routines and beliefs are forming you? What are the well-worn paths you are continually walking?*

....

....

....

....

....

- *What changes would you like to make to your habits, routines and beliefs? What new paths might you want to establish?*

....

....

....

....

....

....

- *What might you need to make these changes?*

....

....

....

....

....

....

- *What specific actions can you take?*

....

....

....

....

....

....

"Would you have a great empire?
Rule over yourself."
~ Publius Syrus ~

26. Make All Conditions Serve You

"To strive, to seek, to find, and not to yield."
~ Alfred Lord Tennyson [1] ~

Make All Conditions Serve You

It is when we put away aimlessness and weakness and think with purpose that we enter the ranks of those strong ones who recognise failure as simply one pathway to attainment. Who make all conditions serve them and who think strongly, attempt fearlessly and accomplish masterfully.

Having set a goal or conceived of a purpose, we should mentally mark out a straight pathway to its achievement, looking neither to the left nor to the right. Doubt and fears should be given no place for they are disintegrating elements that break up the straight line of effort, making it crooked, ineffectual and useless.

Thoughts of doubt and fear never accomplished anything, and never can! They always lead to failure, robbing our strong thoughts of their power, energy and purpose.

Stand guard!

Consider:

It is the very weight of the barbell that causes the muscles to grow as they struggle to lift it. There is no path to fitness or strength that bypasses this struggle. The weight of the barbell and the struggle to lift it is the perfect metaphor for life and is captured beautifully in the Zen proverb *'The obstacle is the path.[2]'*

We cannot grow or build strength without the struggle; the obstacle is the path!

We can, however, choose how we conceptualise the obstacle. We can make it bad, make it a signifier of our failings or we can accept it as part of the growth process. Ryan Holiday, author of the excellent book 'The Obstacle is the Way[3]' puts it like this:

> *"How we approach, view, and contextualize an obstacle, and what we tell ourselves it means, determines how daunting and trying it will be to overcome. It's your choice whether you want to put I in front of something (I hate public speaking. I screwed up. I am harmed by this). These add an extra element: you in relation to that obstacle, rather than just the obstacle itself. And with the wrong perspective, we become consumed and overwhelmed with something actually quite small."*

Instead of fighting the obstacle or shaming yourself because of the obstacle, what if you welcomed it? What if you saw it as the newest piece of equipment in the gym, perfectly designed to develop and enhance your fitness?

Reflect:

Reflect on the following message from Jocko Willink[4], author and retired United States Navy Seal:

"This is something that one of my direct subordinates, one of the guys who worked for me, a guy who became one of my best friends pointed out. He would pull me aside with some major problem or issue that was going on, and he'd say, "Boss, we've got this thing, this situation, and it's going terribly wrong." I would look at him and say, "Good." And finally, one day, he was telling me about something that was going off the rails, and as soon as he finished explaining it to me, he said, "I already know what you're going to say." And I asked, "What am I going to say?" And he said, "You're going to say: 'Good.' " He continued, "That's what you always say. When something is wrong or going bad, you just look at me and say, 'Good.'" And I said, "Well. I mean it. Because that is how I operate." So I explained to him that when things are going bad, there's going to be some good that will come from it.

Oh, the mission got canceled? Good... We can focus on another one. Didn't get the new high-speed gear we wanted? Good... We can keep it simple. Didn't get promoted? Good... More time to get better. Didn't get funded? Good... We own more of the company. Didn't get the job you wanted? Good... Go out, gain more experience, and build a better resume. Got injured? Good... Needed a break from training. Got tapped out? Good... It's better to tap out in training than tap out on the street. Got beat?

Good... We learned. Unexpected problems? Good... We have to figure out a solution.

That's it. When things are going bad: Don't get all bummed out, don't get frustrated. No. Just look at the issue and say: "Good."

Now, I don't mean to say something trite; I'm not trying to sound like Mr. Smiley Positive Guy. That guy ignores the hard truth. That guy thinks a positive attitude will solve problems. It won't. But neither will dwelling on the problem. No. Accept reality, but focus on the solution. Take that issue, take that setback, take that problem, and turn it into something good. Go forward. And, if you are part of a team, that attitude will spread throughout.

Finally: if you can say the word "good," then guess what? It means you're still alive. It means you're still breathing. And if you're still breathing, that means you've still got some fight left in you. So get up, dust off, reload, recalibrate, re-engage – and go out on the attack."

Actions:

What obstacle/s are you facing? List the opportunities within this obstacle.

....

....

....

....

....

....

"There is no education like adversity."
~ Benjamin Disraeli [5] ~

27. The Enemy of Doubt and Fear is Knowledge!

*"You don't teach people to be less afraid,
you teach them to be braver."*
~ Jordan Peterson[1] ~

The Enemy of Doubt and Fear is Knowledge!

The will and drive to do springs from the knowledge we can do!

Doubt and fear are the great enemies of knowledge, and whoever does not put them to death but encourages them defeats themselves at every step.

Whoever has conquered doubt and fear has conquered failure. Their every thought is allied with power, and all difficulties are bravely met and wisely overcome. Their purposes are planted in season and the bloom and bring forth fruit!

Consider:

Tim Keller, Christian writer and former pastor of Redeemer Presbyterian Church in New York City, tells the following story about the connection between fear, thinking and faith[2].

He had noticed a fatty growth on his hip and after showing it to his doctor, his doctor decided that the best course of action was to remove it. However, his doctor took time to reassure him this was a very simple and safe procedure and that he would be better for it. Tim was convinced and set a date with the doctor to come in for the procedure.

Tim recounts feeling great about the procedure, right until he walked into the doctor's surgery and saw the surgical knives! On seeing the knives, doubt crept in, and pretty soon, he had serious misgivings about the whole thing.

We can all be like this, sure of a venture or course of action until reality hits and we have doubts. Going to a gym and getting fit sounds great until the first time you walk out into the gym and don't really know what any of the machines do! Going back to school to get the qualification you need sounds like a great idea until you arrive at the first class and realise you are at least 15 years older than everyone else.

Having plans is great, but facing up to reality can be something different. So, what do we do? How do we defeat doubt and fear? How do we walk out our plans?

If we return to Tim Keller and his minor operation, we learn something important. Tim recalls seeing the knives and feeling the doubt and fear creep in, but then, upon recognising this he took a specific, active step to address it. He called to mind all the reasons he had for undergoing surgery, he remembered all the doctor's assurances that the surgery was safe and very straightforward. What he did was combat fear and doubt with thinking, with knowledge!

When we feel afraid or when doubt gnaws at our resolve, we can think!

Action:

As you go about your week, pay attention to your feelings of doubt and/or fear. When you notice you are experiencing these feelings, stop and name them, for example:

- *"I am feeling scared."*

Where possible, add as much detail as you can. For example:

- *"I am feeling scared that I will look stupid in the gym because I don't know how the machines work."*

- *"I am beginning to doubt my ability to get this qualification because all of the other people on this course are so much younger than me."*

Once you have done this, spend some deliberate time thinking about your reasons for achieving this goal. When you are ready, acknowledge the feelings of fear and/or doubt and then plan for moving forward, for example:

- *"I will ask one of the staff members to show me how three of the machines work and I'll work out on them today."*

"With the exercise of self-trust,
new powers shall appear."
~ Ralph Waldo Emerson [3] ~

28. Creative Force

"He who has a 'why' to live for can bear almost any how."
~ Friedrich Nietzsche [1] ~

A Creative Force

Thought, when allied fearlessly to purpose, becomes a creative force.

Whoever knows this is ready to become something higher and stronger than a mere bundle of wavering thoughts and fluctuating sensations.

Whoever does this has become the conscious and intelligent wielder of their mental powers.

Consider:

In his TEDTalk, 'Start with Why', Simon Sinek[2] presents a fascinating approach to connecting our actions to our purpose, which he calls 'The Golden Circle'.

'Why' is at the centre of the diagram followed by 'how' and then 'what'. Sinek suggests that almost every business, organisation and individual knows and understands their 'what'; this is 'what I/we do.' The 'what' can be as simple as 'I'm a stay-at-home dad and I look after the kids, that's what I do' or as complex as 'Our organisation provides tailored IT systems to manage the ordering and distribution of product.'

He states that almost every business, organisation and individual understands 'how' they do 'what' they do.

"I get up before the kids to make breakfast for them. On Tuesday mornings, we go to the library."

Sinek argues, however, that many businesses, organisations and individuals don't know 'why' they do 'what' they do. Outcomes such as 'making money' or 'because the kids like the library', he argues, are results that are different from purpose. Why do you take your kids to the library? Or better yet, why did you choose to be a stay-at-home dad? What is your purpose in this?

Understanding your 'why' is connecting to your purpose.

When we understand our purpose, when we can talk about it and clearly describe it, we are better equipped to make choices that helps us to live in closer alignment with the actions and beliefs we value.

"Fulfilment comes from having a clear sense of purpose for what we do. From knowing 'why' we do what we do."
~ Simon Sinek [2] ~

Actions:

In the box below, reflect on your 'why' (you may have more than one!). Remember, this differs from describing what you do or how you do it.

"It's not enough to have lived.
We should be determined to live for something."
~ Winston Churchilln [3] ~

It's time to get creative! In the second box, consider how you can more consistently live in alignment with your why/s.

"People who use time wisely spend it on activities that advance their overall purpose in life."
~ John C. Maxwell [4] ~

29. The Thought-Factor in Achievement

"My sense is that if you want to change the world, you start with yourself and work outward because you build your competence that way."
~ Jordan Peterson [1] ~

The Thought-Factor in Achievement

All that a man achieves and all that he fails to achieve results directly from his thoughts.

In a justly ordered universe, where loss of balance would mean total destruction, individual responsibility must be absolute.

Our weakness and strength, purity and impurity are our own and not another's, we bring them about and not another and they can be altered only when we do something.

Our conditions are also our own and not another's.

Likewise, our suffering and happiness also evolve from within.

So, as we think we are and as we continue to think, so we remain!

Consider:
This passage needs to be read sensibly. Clearly, the suffering experienced by a parent as they watch their child undergo a painful procedure has not 'evolved from within'. However, individuals can experience very similar situations and yet 'suffer' to greater or lesser extents. There is the 'suffering' contained within the event, and then there is the 'suffering' that we bring forth from within. Amy Purdy is an excellent example of this reality.

At 19 years old, Amy lost both legs below the knee due to a severe case of bacterial meningitis. This event undoubtedly caused suffering, losing one leg would be traumatic, but both is hard to comprehend. Additionally, this suffering did not 'evolve from within' but was part and parcel of the trauma. And yet Amy got to a point in her recovery where she realized that any further suffering would no longer come solely from the trauma, but also from within, from the story she was telling. During an interview with Oprah, she recounts realizing that she was the author of her story and that it was up to her to write a happy one! In this moment, she moved into a new phase, taking responsibility for the story of her life, choosing not to suffer but to thrive.

Amy has since won a bronze medal in the 2014 Winter Paralympics and was featured on the American TV show 'Dancing with Stars'[2].

"...as we think we are; and as we continue to think, so we remain!"

Action:

Tony Robbins suggests that suffering can often result from one of three patterns of thinking: *less, loss & never*[3] and it is easy to see these three patterns within Amy's story: she lost the use of her legs, leaving her with fewer options, perhaps making less likely to succeed or find happiness and there are certainly many things may now feel like they will never happen, such as going dancing or enjoying buying shoes!

By taking responsibility for her thinking, Amy changed her experience of her situation. The situation hadn't changed, but Amy had!

Think of a challenge you are facing or a situation in your life causing you pain. List the stories that you are currently telling yourself about this situation/challenge underneath the following three headings

Less

....

....

....

....

....

....

Loss

....

....

....

....

....

....

Never

....

....

....

....

....

....

Having captured your thoughts, now consider the following three headings:

Gratitude: *What can you appreciate and enjoy?*

Growth: *How can you learn and grow through this?*

Give: *What would it look like to love, give and be grateful?*

What can you appreciate and enjoy?

....

....

....

....

....

....

How can you learn and grow through this?

....

....

....

....

....

....

What would it look like to love, give and be grateful?

....

....

....

....

....

....

30. Claiming our Strength

"There is no greater agony than bearing an untold story inside you."
~ Maya Angelou [1] ~

Claiming our Strength

A strong person is not enough to truly help a weak person, for the weak person must be willing to be helped and this willingness to be helped must give way to the formation of inner strength to help themself. Without this inner growth, when the strong person leaves, the weak person is shown to be weak once more. Truly then, none but the individual can ever alter their condition.

A person can only rise, conquer, and achieve by lifting up their thoughts and will surely remain weak, abject and miserable by refusing to lift up their thoughts.

Before we can achieve anything, even at the simple level, we must lift up our thoughts above slavish and animal indulgence. A person whose first thought is base and indulgent will never think clearly nor plan methodically. They will not discover their potential, their inner genius, and will fail in any undertaking.

We must undertake a concerted effort to control and master our thoughts, and until we have done this, we are not ready to control affairs and adopt serious responsibilities. The world does not impose these limitations on us. Rather, they are the natural consequences of our thoughts. Our thoughts limit us.

Consider:

Alfred Lickspittle is an adviser to the Master of Lake-Town in the recent 'Hobbit' movie franchise[2]. He is a weasel of a man, happy to throw his weight around and delighted by the power afforded him by his position. As the film progresses, Alfred's corrupted character becomes ever more evident as he sneaks and lies and hides.

The thing that interests me about Alfred is that despite other characters saving him from dangers such as a dragon, warrior trolls and angry villagers, no one is ultimately able to save Alfred from himself and when the film ends, Alfred has slunk away dressed as an old woman carrying as much gold as he can stuff into his bra! The thing that Alfred needed rescuing from to truly save him wasn't a dragon or a troll but weak and selfish thoughts.

Interestingly Jordan Peterson, author, clinical psychologist and professor of psychology at the University of Toronto, suggests that the rescue required in situations such as this comes not from a heroic outsider (although this can be helpful) but from the individual taking responsibility. 'Most people', Peterson writes, 'find meaning in their life through responsibility', while not taking responsivity paves the road to 'self-disgust, self-contempt and shame.'

Consider the following extract from an interview with Peterson[3]:

"Life is very difficult. It will challenge you to your core. You need to be able to withstand that challenge or you'll warp and deteriorate. How do you develop yourself to withstand

that challenge? You take on responsibilities and challenges voluntarily and strengthen yourself. How else could you possibly do it? You could hide, but there's no hiding. You can't hide from illness and death. You can't hide from loneliness or pain. It's not possible. If you retreat, then the things that chase you just grow larger. You have to put yourself together, and you do that by seeing what's right in front of you, regardless of whether or not you like it, and encouraging yourself to master what you see voluntarily and to extend yourself and to stretch yourself out constantly. You do that with your eyes open, and you do that with your speech and thinking carefully monitored and regulated so that you don't corrupt yourself with unnecessary ignorance and delusion, because that will just hurt you when the crisis comes.

The goal of authenticity from an existential perspective is to pursue that which you could be so that you can flesh yourself out, so you can burn off what about you is dead and outdated and so that you can allow what could be to come to life. The deep archetypal idea is that to the degree that you do that, you redeem yourself and you redeem the world around you. Again, I don't think that that's metaphysics. It seems to be the most practical of truths. The archetype, for example, the hero archetype, you could say what it is it's that which you find admirable."

Action:

Step back and think of your life as movie you are watching with you in the lead role. Now answer these questions:

What role is your character playing?

....
....
....
....
....
....

What role could your character play?

....
....
....
....
....
....

How would you like your story to end?

....

....

....

....

....

....

What is the problem that has to be overcome?

....

....

....

....

....

....

What do you need to learn to overcome this problem?

....

....

....

....

....

....

What current pattern of thinking would prevent this?

....

....

....

....

....

....

What do you need to you take responsibility for to move the story forward?

....

....

....

....

....

....

"There is no greater agony
than bearing an untold story inside you."
~ Maya Angelou ~

31. The Rewards of Right Thinking

"Finally, brothers and sisters, whatever is true, whatever is noble, whatever is right, whatever is pure, whatever is lovely, whatever is admirable—if anything is excellent or praiseworthy—think about such things."
~ St. Paul [1] ~

The Rewards of Right Thinking

The Universe does not favour the greedy, the dishonest or the vicious, although on the surface, it may sometimes appear to do so. Rather, it helps the honest, the magnanimous and the virtuous. All the great teachers have declared this in varying forms, and to prove and know it a person has but to persist in making themself more and more virtuous by lifting up their thoughts.

Intellectual achievements result from thoughts given to the search for knowledge or for the beautiful and true in life and nature. These achievements may be connected with vanity and ambition, but they are not the outcomes of these characteristics. They are rather the natural outgrowth of long and arduous effort and of pure and unselfish thoughts.

Spiritual achievements are the realisation of right and pure aspiration. Whoever meditates upon all that is pure and unselfish and engages in the deliberate rehearsal of noble and good thoughts, will, as surely as the sun rises, become wise and noble in character, rising into positions of influence and blessedness.

Achievement of every kind is the result and natural outcome of efforts in right thinking.

It is through self-control, dedication, purity, uprightness and well-directed thought that we ascend and through laziness, corruption, indulgence of lesser desires and confusion of thought that we descend.

Do not lose sight of the seed which produced the harvest. All achievements, whether in the business, intellectual or inner world result from definitely directed thought. Victories accomplished by right-thinking can be maintained only by watchfulness. Many lose their focus when success comes and rapidly fall back into failure.

In the law of sowing and reaping, there is always work to be done. Whoever would accomplish little must sacrifice little; whoever would achieve much must sacrifice much and whoever would attain highly must sacrifice greatly.

Consider:

For the first time in my working career, I had a day off outside of school holidays. Until now, I had always worked in schools, but today, on this glorious day, I was off while the world around me worked.

Having packed a bag with a portable stove and coffee pot, I headed out to the glens towards Loch Wharral. The snow was gently falling as I set off, making the climb even more beautiful than normal, but soon, my legs were burning. Not only was the climb steeper than I had anticipated, but this was one of those mountains with false summits, so you were never sure how far you still had to go.

During one of my many breaks, as I stopped to catch my breath and rest my legs a little, a thought occurred; the solution to summiting this climb wasn't complicated, I just had to follow the path and not stop. If I continued with these actions, summiting would be inevitable! Granted, I didn't know when I would summit, but I did know without a shadow of a doubt I would!

Summiting became inevitable!

Reflect:

"I passed by the field of a sluggard, by the vineyard of a man lacking sense, and behold, it was all overgrown with thorns; the ground was covered with nettles, and its stone wall was broken down. Then I saw and considered it; I looked and received instruction. A little sleep, a little slumber, a little folding of the hands to rest, and poverty will come upon you like a robber, and want like an armed man.
~ Proverbs 24: 30 – 34 [2] ~

- Victory is often achieved through the accumulation of small advancements.

- Disaster is often the product of the accumulation of small submissions.

Actions:

- What mountain are you climbing?

....

....

....

....

....

....

- What actions would make summiting inevitable?

....

....

....

....

....

....

- What rituals could you create so these behaviours become a normal part of your everyday life?

....

....

....

....

....

....

"Do not lose sight of the seed which produced the harvest."

32. Visions & Ideals

"Whatever you can do, or dream you can do, begin it.
Boldness has genius, magic, and power in it.
Begin it now."
~ Johann Wolfgang von Goethe [1] ~

Visions & Ideals

The dreamers are the saviours of this world, for just as the visible world is sustained by the invisible, so we are nourished through our trials, failings and shameful pursuits by the beautiful visions of these solitary dreamers. Humanity cannot forget its dreamers; it cannot let their ideals fade and die, for we live in them, gaining strength from the belief that one day their dreams will be made true.

We need the dreamers. We need the reminder that what is dreamt of and cherished in the heart can be made real! Columbus cherished a vision of another world and did discover it. Copernicus nurtured the vision of a multiplicity of worlds and a wider universe and revealed it to be so!

Cherish your visions; cherish your ideals; cherish the music that stirs in your heart, the beauty that forms in your mind, the liveliness that colours your purest thoughts, for out of them will grow all delightful conditions.

To desire is to obtain; to aspire is to achieve. But what is the seed that is nurtured? Do we tend and care for our basest desire for surely this will be the harvest we reap. We might talk of great things, but in the garden of our minds tend harmful and defeating thoughts. We must lift our thoughts from these low things and dream lofty dreams, for as we dream so shall we become. Our vision is the promise of what we shall one day be; our ideal is the prophecy of what we shall at last unveil.

What power is there in a dream, you might ask. Consider the mighty oak tree that sleeps within the acorn or the powerful eagle that waits within the egg. Our dreams are powerful for they are the seedlings of the realities we would bring forth.

Consider:

"We need the reminder that that which is dreamt of and cherished in the heart can be made real!"

Through what mechanism are dreams made real? Swiss psychiatrist Carl Jung offers a deeply helpful insight into this process, suggesting that the savior must always be preceded by the fool[2]. What does this mean? Simply that unless you are willing to become a beginner, to do a thing poorly and risk looking a fool, you cannot become more than you are now. The fool precedes the savior.

When I used to train Ju Jitsu, our coach would express this same idea through the phrase *'You have to be the nail before you get to be the hammer',* and boy, was that the truth! Week after week, I'd feel the fool as everyone in the gym would submit me. Worse than that was the uncomfortable knowledge I was everyone's easy round; I was the practice dummy. But redemption also came through this route; over time, I grew in skill, becoming more than I was. Slowly but surely, it took my opponents longer to submit me, I saw the traps, I even mounted a few attacks of my own. The fool slowly gave way to something more. I slowly became something more.

In the words of Elizabeth Gilbert[3], *"...this, I believe, is the central question upon which all creative living hinges: Do you have the courage to bring forth the treasures that are hidden within you?"* Are you courageous enough to embrace being foolish?

Actions:

What vision/s do you cherish?

....

....

....

....

....

....

"To desire is to obtain, to aspire is to achieve. But what is the seed that is nurtured?"

What seeds are you nurturing?

....

....

....

....

....

....

"We need the reminder that that which is dreamt of and cherished in the heart can be made real!"

What first steps can you take to make your dreams real?

....

....

....

....

....

....

What learning for you is there in Jung's concept of the fool preceding the saviour?

....

....

....

....

....

....

What will you do with this learning?

....

....

....

....

....

....

"So this, I believe, is the central question upon which all creative living hinges: Do you have the courage to bring forth the treasures that are hidden within you?"
~ Elizabeth Gilbert ~

33. You cannot travel within and stand still without!

"It is only when a man tames his own demons that he becomes the king of himself if not of the world."
~ Joseph Campbell [1] ~

You cannot travel within and stand still without!

What of circumstance, what of opportunity? They may oppose you or be few and far between, but this will not long remain so when we create an ideal in our mind and strive to reach it.

You cannot travel within and stand still without!

We will always gravitate towards that which we most love and into our hands will be placed the exact results of our own thoughts.

Whatever your present environment may be, you will fall, remain or rise in accordance with your thoughts, your vision and your ideal. You will become as small or as great as your most frequent thought!

Consider:

"You cannot travel within and stand still without!"

Bilbo Baggins, the lead character in J. R. R. Tolkien's wonderful book 'The Hobbit'[2], is anything but your typical adventurer; he is short, timid and soft. Yet by the end of the book, he has stolen a priceless treasure from beneath a sleeping dragon. Bilbo's adventure is geographical, taking him from his home to the far away Misty Mountains. However, had his adventure only been geographical, he would have arrived at the Misty Mountains without the inner resources to enter the dragon's lair, unearth the treasure and complete the quest. Before entering the dragon's cave, Bilbo enters the dark places within himself, seeking those treasures buried within.

Our lives are testament to the fact that the 'treasure' found in new geographical locations (a new job, a new gym, a new school, a new house, a new relationship) rarely contain the transformative power of the 'treasure' buried within us. It is easy to think of those individuals who continually move from job to job, relationship to relationship, town to town, seeking externally what is buried within themselves should they look. Yet much like Bilbo's adventure, a dragon guards the treasure within and must be faced before the treasure can be brought forth.

Carl Jung famously noted, "that which we need the most will be found where we least want to look.[3]" Information, treasure, resides within us that will aid us if only we are brave enough to look.

You cannot undertake work of this manner without change; you cannot travel within and stand still without!

Actions:

What inner journey do you need to take? Note, this isn't an opportunity to revisit old wounds to further blame, shame or judge yourself, but to visit as an explorer, an investigator to discover what valuable information can be found.

What can you learn about yourself?

What valuable insight can be unearthed?

Be mindful this insight may well necessitate the 'death' of aspects of your personality. However, this death may well facilitate liberating rebirth.

What inner journey do I need to take?

....

....

....

....

....

....

What treasure resides there? (What can I learn?)

....

....

....

....

....

How can I respond to this new information?

....

....

....

....

....

Do I notice any other areas within me that are 'off limit'?

....

....

....

....

....

*"It's a dangerous business, Frodo, going out your door.
You step onto the road, and if you don't keep your feet,
there's no knowing where you might be swept off to."*
~ J.R.R. Tolkien [4] ~

34. The Thoughts we Become

"You may encounter many defeats, but you must not be defeated. In fact, it may be necessary to encounter the defeats, so you can know who you are, what you can rise from, how you can still come out of it."
~ Maya Angelou [1] ~

The Thoughts we Become

Do not be like the thoughtless, ignorant and lazy who only see the effects of things and not the things themselves. They show their foolishness in their talk of luck, fortune or change. Seeing a person grow rich, they call it luck, observing another become wise, they say, "How privileged!" Observing the upright character and influence of another, they remark, "How chance aids them at every turn!"

These people are fools, for they do not see the trials, failures and struggles which these others have voluntarily encountered in order to gain what they possess. They have no knowledge of the sacrifices made, the undaunted efforts put forth or the intense exercise of faith undertaken to overcome the apparently insurmountable.

They do not know the darkness and the heartaches; they only see the light and joy and call it luck! They do not see the long and arduous journey, but only see the pleasant outcome and call it good fortune. They do not understand the process, but only perceive the result and call it change!

There are efforts and there are results and the strength of the effort is the measure of the result. Chance is not.

Gifts, powers, material, intellectual and spiritual possessions are the fruits of effort. They are thoughts completed, objects accomplished, visions realised!

The vision you glorify in your mind, the ideal you enthrone in your heart – this you will build your life by, this you will become.

Consider:

There are two simple images I think about often when reflecting on success and failure. The first shows two individuals with their failures represented as boxes. Both individuals have collected a large number of these 'failure boxes'. However, while the first character has chosen to pile the boxes on top of himself, weighing himself down, the second character is using her 'failure boxes' to construct a staircase.

The second image depicts three athletes standing on the 1st, 2nd and 3rd place positions on a podium. In front of them is a crowd of cheering fans and news reporters who have observed their successful performances and are celebrating them. However, hidden from view and sitting beneath the podium are the unseen building blocks that led to the athletes' success. These building blocks have titles such as 'hard work', 'sacrifice', 'pain and discomfort', 'discipline' and 'patience'.

Ryan Holiday, author of the fantastic book 'The Obstacle is the Way'[2] captures both of these images in the following observation:

"Many people think genius is a moment of inspiration, it isn't! It's the slow pressure, the constant chipping away, the elimination of so many other options. Genius, as it turns out, looks a lot like persistence in disguise."

Consider these examples:

Henry Ford

Bankrupt five times in other businesses before succeeding with the Ford Motor Company.

Walt Disney

Fired from his first job at the Kansas City Star because his cartoons weren't creative enough.

Albert Einstein

Didn't talk until he was four or read until he was seven. His parents and teachers thought he was mentally handicapped.

Steven King

His first novel 'Carrie' was rejected by publishers 30 times.

Jack Canfield & Mark Victor

The 'Chicken Soup for the Soul' authors pitched their book idea to over 130 publishers. After 100 rejections, they were dropped by their agent. Their book has now sold over 500 million copies sold.

Jack Ma

Jack applied to and was rejected by Harvard 10 times. He founded the online store Alibaba and became the richest man in Asia.

Sir James Dyson:

Dyson took 5126 attempts to produce a working bagless vacuum cleaner. The Dyson Corporation is now worth more than £3 billion.

"Most of the important things in the world have been accomplished by people who have kept on trying when there seemed to be no hope at all."
~ Dale Carnegie [3] ~

Actions:

Over the coming days, pay attention to how you are using your failures and the effect this is having on you.

What steps can you take to move toward the approach shown on the right of this image?

....

....

....

....

....

....

"Perseverance, secret of all triumphs."
~ Victor Hugo [4] ~

35. Serenity

"When a problem is disturbing you, don't ask,
"What should I do about it?"
Ask, "What part of me is being disturbed by this?"
~ Michael A. Singer [1] ~

Serenity

Calmness of mind is one of the beautiful jewels of wisdom. It results from long and patient effort in self-control. Its presence is a sign of individual maturity and insight into the laws and operations of thought.

A person becomes calm to the extent that they understand that their condition results from thought. Such knowledge makes clear the cause-and-effect relationships that govern our world and enables us to stop our fussing and worry and grief and to instead remain steadfast, stable and at peace.

Consider:

Serenity is not a life without problems, nor is it a forced insistence that things 'aren't really that bad'. Rather, like an ocean whose surface can be violently tossed and churned by the storm, serenity is the stillness that resides below the waves.

In the quote at the start of this chapter, Michael Singer presents a strategy for accessing the serenity available within. According to Singer, asking 'what part of me is disturbed by this' allows us to observe the problem and separate ourselves from it. Untangling ourselves from the problem is the first step in moving from the turbulent surface of the storm and into the stillness beneath. This can be thought of as moving from looking 'from' the problem *"I'm always going to be this sick!"* to looking 'at' the problem

"I notice that part of me is scared that I'll always be this sick and I'm curious about that." Standing witness to the problem, to use Singer's language, separates us from the problem. While we are witness to it, we aren't 'it' and, as such, can move away from it.

This is a realistic approach to the challenges we face, fully acknowledging there will be problems in our lives and that many will be deeply painful. However, beneath the surface of the storm, stillness is available and we can learn to access it.

Carl Rogers[2], the famous American psychologist, presents a similar view of the utility of self-awareness as a psychological tool for disentangling self from the current challenge, he writes:

> *"The term 'congruent' is one I have used to describe the way I would like to be. By this I mean that whatever feeling or attitude I am experiencing would be matched by my awareness of that attitude. When this is true, then I am a unified or integrated person in that moment, and hence I can be whatever I deeply am."*

By asking 'what part of me is disturbed by this', we raise awareness of the inner disturbance we are feeling. While this doesn't magically make the challenge disappear, it does allow us to exist as an 'integrated person' within a storm, but able to move away from the violent surface and into the calmer depths below.

Actions:

During the next few weeks, make use of the following two strategies as deliberate attempts to access the serenity that exists beneath the surface of the storm.

One:

- Look 'at' your problem rather than 'from' your problem. This creates separation and distance. For example:

- Looking from *"I'll never manage this!"*

- Looking at *"I notice that I'm telling myself that I'll never manage."*

Two:

Having achieved separation from the problem, develop the habit of asking 'what part of me is disturbed by this?' and then carefully and lovingly consider what that part of you might need.

"There is nothing more important to true growth than realizing that you are not the voice of the mind - you are the one who hears it."
~ Michael A. Singer [1] ~

36. The Calm, Steady State

*"Be like the promontory against which the waves
continually break, but it stands firm and tames the fury
of the water around it."*
~ Marcus Aurelius [1] ~

The Calm, Steady State

Having learned to govern ourselves, creating an inner calm, we learn how to adapt ourselves to others. Experiencing our calm and steady state, those around us respond to our inner strength becoming more willing to learn from us and rely on us.

The more tranquil a person becomes, the more consistently they manage themselves, the greater their success, influence, and power for good. Even the most ordinary person will find their wellbeing and success increase as they grow in self-control and composure, for people prefer to deal with those whose conduct is steady and consistent.

The strong, calm person is always loved and admired. They are like a shade-giving tree in a thirsty land or a sheltering rock in a storm. Who does not love a tranquil heart, a sweet-tempered, balanced life? It does not matter whether it rains or shines or what changes come to those possessing these blessings, for they are always sweet, serene, and calm.

That exquisite poise of character, which we call serenity, is the last lesson of accomplishment, the harvest of the soul. It is precious as wisdom, more to be desired than gold. How insignificant the pursuit of money looks in comparison with a serene life--a life that dwells in the ocean of Truth, beneath the waves, beyond the reach of tempests, in the Eternal Calm!

Consider

Shelters offer protection from the environment by shielding us from the weather outside. Within a shelter, it is possible to be aware of the weather, to hear the battering of the rain and the blowing of the wind, and yet be untouched by them.

Maxwell Maltz, the author of 'Psycho-Cybernetics'[2], suggests that tranquilizers can be thought of as psychic shelters providing a barrier between the external stimuli and the individual. The tranquilized individual can still recognize external stimuli intellectually, they no longer respond to them emotionally. The tranquillity produced by tranquilizers is not a consequence of removing the external stimulus but in stopping or reducing the internal response.

Tranquilizers, Maltz argues, offer convincing evidence that our internal state is largely determined by our response to the world. Tranquilizers also speak to the availability of psyche shelter, consider the following quote from Marcus Aurelius[1]:

> "Men seek retreats for themselves: houses in the country, sea-shores and mountains and thou too art wont to desire such things very much, but this is altogether a mark of the most common sort of men, for is in thy power whenever thou shalt choose to retire into thyself. For nowhere, either with more quiet or more freedom from trouble, does a man retire than into his own soul, particularly when he has within him such thoughts that by looking into them he is immediately in perfect tranquillity and I affirm that tranquillity is nothing else than the good ordering of the mind.

Constantly then give thyself this retreat and renew thyself!"

President Truman famously made use of this inner retreat during World War II, stating that just as soldiers retreat into a foxhole for protection, rest and recuperation, so too he had a foxhole in his mind in which he could find peace from the situations surrounding him.

Actions:

Use your imagination to build a quiet room in your mind. Decorate this room with whatever furnishing is most restful and relaxing for you. Spend some time creating a room you find both peaceful and beautiful. Lastly, choose a view that speaks to your soul, such as mountains, the ocean or a quiet forest.

Over the next week, practice visiting this room, taking time to imagine walking up to the door to the room, removing your cares and worries and leaving them outside as you venture in. Enjoy looking at the room you have made before mindfully settling into your comfy chair. Picture in your mind's eye the view you have chosen, feeling your muscles relax as you enjoy the beauty before you.

As you become more practised in this habit, you will find you can enter this quiet room and this state of peace with greater ease. Your peaceful room will be available to you between emails, at traffic jams, on your lunch break and as you fall asleep.

"Be like the promontory against which the waves continually break, but it stands firm and tames the fury of the water around it."
~ Marcus Aurelius ~

37. The Finished Character

"If you wanna be somebody
If you wanna go somewhere
You better wake up and pay attention."
~ Sister Act 2: Back in the Habit [1] ~

The Finished Character

"How many people we know who sour their lives,

Who ruin all that is sweet and beautiful

by explosive tempers,

Who destroy their poise of character,

and make bad blood!

It is a question of whether the great majority of people do not ruin their lives

And mar their happiness by lack of self-control.

How few people do we meet in life

who are well balanced,

Who have that exquisite poise which is characteristic of the finished character!"

Humanity surges and boils with uncontrolled passion, is tumultuous with ungoverned grief, is blown about by anxiety and doubt. But not so the wise person. Their thoughts are controlled and purified, so make the winds and the storms of the soul obey them.

Storm-tossed souls, wherever you may be, under whatsoever conditions you may live, know this, in the ocean of life, the isles of Blessedness are smiling, and the sunny shore of your ideal awaits your coming.

Keep your hand firmly upon the helm of thought. Asleep in your soul reclines the commanding Master; wake Him!

Self-control is strength.

Right-Thought is mastery.

Calmness is power.

Say unto your heart, "Peace, be still!"

Consider:

> *"If you wanna be somebody*
>
> *If you wanna go somewhere*
>
> *You better wake up and pay attention."*
>
> ~ Sister Act 2: Back in the Habit ~

As I reflect on this book, it is to my great amusement that a song from the 1993 movie 'Sister Act 2: Back in the Habit' appears to capture many of the key ideas discussed: wake up, pay attention, take responsibility and act.

Hopefully, as you have read this book, you have experienced many moments of insight, of waking up and seeing. Yet, while insights are valuable, it is all too easy to once again fall asleep, to close our eyes to the routines we fall into and to allow our thoughts to go unnoticed. Waking up and staying awake is hard to do and this thought leads us to another unexpected source of wisdom upon which to draw this book to a close, Mr Arnold Schwarzenegger, who said the following when describing the process of growth and improvement:

*"There are no shortcuts,
everything is reps, reps, reps."*

~ Arnold Schwarzenegger [2] ~

Friends, there is work to do, there are no shortcuts, but you were made to do this! When fed correctly, your body is made to grow strong as it works, so to your spirit! Wake up! Pay Attention and put the reps in! You were made for this!

Actions:
Make a plan to help you stay awake.
This may involve scheduling regular check-ins with yourself to review your habits and routines.

Remember, the purpose of this plan is not to beat yourself up for falling back asleep, but to develop the habit of being awake.

What will you do?

....

....

....

....

....

*"If you wanna be somebody
If you wanna go somewhere
You better wake up and pay attention."*

~ Sister Act 2: Back in the Habit ~

Notes

Preface

1. Taleb, N. N. (2012). *Antifragile: Things that gain from disorder* (Vol. 3). Random House Incorporated.
2. Allen, J. (2003). *As a man thinketh*. Holmes Book Company.

Chapter 1

1. Tolle, E. (2004). *The power of now: A guide to spiritual enlightenment*. New World Library.
2. Tolle, E. (2009). *A new earth: create a better life*. Penguin UK.
3. Carnegie, D. (2021). *How to stop worrying and start living*. Meltem Toker.

Chapter 2

1. The Taboo Trifecta (2017) Freakonomics, 1st March. Available at: https://freakonomics.com/podcast/the-taboo-trifecta/ (Accessed: 17 December 2021).
2. Syed, M. (2010). *Bounce: The myth of talent and the power of practice*. HarperCollins UK.
3. Ericsson, K. A., & Harwell, K. W. (2019). Deliberate practice and proposed limits on the effects of practice on the acquisition of expert performance: Why the original definition matters and

recommendations for future research. *Frontiers in psychology*, *10*, 2396.

4. Gandhi, M. K. (2018). *The story of my experiments with truth: An autobiography*. Om Books International.

Chapter 3

1. Covey, S. R. (2004). *The 7 habits of highly effective people: Powerful lessons in personal change*. Simon and Schuster.

2. Ferris, T. (November 2016) *Tools of Titans: Derek Sivers Distilled (#202)*. Available at: https://tim.blog/2016/11/21/tools-of-titans-derek-sivers-distilled/ (Accessed: 17 December 2021).

3. Frankl, V. E. (1985). *Man's search for meaning*. Simon and Schuster.

Chapter 4

1. Rohn, J. (2017) *The Ultimate Jim Rohn Library. Narrated by Jim Rohn.* Available at: https://www.audible.co.uk/pd/The-Ultimate-Jim-Rohn-Library-Audiobook/B076PRHZSD (Accessed: 17 December 2021).

Chapter 5

2. Campbell, J. (2017). *A Joseph Campbell companion: Reflections on the art of living*. Joseph Campbell Foundation.

3. Jung, C. G. (2014). Aion Christ, A Symbol of the Self. In *Collected Works of CG Jung, Volume 9 (Part 2)* (pp. 36-71). Princeton University Press.

4. Gilbert, E. (2016). *Big magic: Creative living beyond fear*. Penguin.

Chapter 6

1. Smiles, S. (1887). *Life and Labour: or, characteristics of men of industry, culture and genius* (Vol. 33). London: J. Murray.

2. TED (2013) *What I learned from Nelson Mandela*. December 2013. Available at: https://www.ted.com/talks/boyd_varty_what_i_lea rned_from_nelson_mandela?language=en#t-179379 (Accessed: 17 December 2021).

3. Ferriss, T. (2017). *Tools of Titans: The Tactics, Routines, and Habits of Billionaires, Icons, and World-Class Performers*. Houghton Mifflin.

4. Jay, W. M. L. (ed.) (2013) *The More Abundant Life: Lenten Readings, Selected Chiefly from Unpublished Manuscripts of the Rt. Rev. Phillips Brooks*. HardPress Publishing

5. Henley, W. E. (1995). Invictus. *Përpjekja*, (03), 78-79.

Chapter 7

1. This quote is widely attributed to Barbara Myerhoff. I cannot locate the original text from which the quote is taken.

Chapter 8

1. Emerson, R. W. (2003). *The conduct of life* (Vol. 6). Harvard University Press.
2. Roosevelt, T. (1920). *American ideals*. GP Putnam.

Chapter 9

1. Rohn, J. (2017) *The Ultimate Jim Rohn Library. Narrated by Jim Rohn.* Available at: https://www.audible.co.uk/pd/The-Ultimate-Jim-Rohn-Library-Audiobook/B076PRHZSD (Accessed: 17 December 2021).
2. Achor, S. (2011). *The happiness advantage: The seven principles of positive psychology that fuel success and performance at work*. Random House.

Chapter 10

1. Johnson, S. (1785). *The rambler* (Vol. 1). Harrison and Company.
2. Business Insider Australia (2015) *This hugely popular author shares her 'number one life hack' for resilient relationships.* Available at: https://www.businessinsider.com.au/brene-browns-biggest-life-hack-is-a-simple-phrase-2015-8 (Accessed: 18 December 2021).

Chapter 11

1. Pressfield, S. (2002). *The war of art: Break through the blocks and win your inner creative battles*. Black Irish Entertainment LLC.

Chapter 12

1. Beecher, H. W. (1858). *Life thoughts*. J. Blackwood.
2. Murphy, J. (2019) *The Power Of Your Subconscious Mind*. London: Simon & Schuster

Chapter 13

1. Headspace (no date) 33 of the Best Meditation Quotes. Available at: https://www.headspace.com/meditation/quotes (Accessed: 22 December 2021).

2. Pakenham, K.I. and Rinaldis, M., 2001. The role of illness, resources, appraisal, and coping strategies in adjustment to HIV/AIDS: The direct and buffering effects. *Journal of Behavioral Medicine*, *24*(3), pp.259-279.

3. Stanton, A.L., Tennen, H., Affleck, G. and Mendola, R., 1991. Cognitive appraisal and adjustment to infertility. *Women & Health*, *17*(3), pp.1-15.

4. Gass, K.A. and Chang, A.S., 1989. Appraisals of bereavement, coping, resources, and psychosocial health dysfunction in widows and widowers. *Nursing Research*.

Chapter 14

1. Disraeli, B. (1844). *Coningsby: or, the new generation* (Vol. 67). B. Tauchnitz.

2. Covey, S. R. (2004). *The 7 habits of highly effective people: Powerful lessons in personal change*. Simon and Schuster.

Chapter 15

1. New Statesman (2014) *Winston Churchill interviewed in 1939: "The British people would rather go down fighting"*. Available at: https://www.newstatesman.com/uncategorized/2014/01/british-people-would-rather-go-down-fighting (Accessed: 18 December 2021).
2. Graham, B. (2007). *Just as I am: The autobiography of Billy Graham*. Zondervan.
3. Peale, N. V. (2012). *The power of positive thinking*. Random House.
4. Emerson, R. W. (1982). *Emerson in his Journals*. Harvard University Press.

Chapter 16

1. There are a number of authors associated with this quote. American novelist Brad Thor is reported to have said this when describing his approach to writing. However, both Tony Robbins and Rim Rohn are also known for teaching this principle.
2. Durant, W. (1961). *Story of philosophy*. Simon and Schuster.

Chapter 17

1. This quote is attributed to Mark Twain. However, in recent years this has been questioned. See the following for more info: https://quoteinvestigator.com/2013/10/04/never-happened/
2. *About Time* (2013) Directed by Richard Curtis [Feature Film]. United Kingdom: Working Title Films
3. Ferriss, T. (2017). *Tools of Titans: The Tactics, Routines, and Habits of Billionaires, Icons, and World-Class Performers*. Houghton Mifflin.

Chapter 18

1. Rohn, J. (2017) *The Ultimate Jim Rohn Library. Narrated by Jim Rohn*. Available at: https://www.audible.co.uk/pd/The-Ultimate-Jim-Rohn-Library-Audiobook/B076PRHZSD (Accessed: 17 December 2021).
2. Covey, S. R. (2004). *The 7 habits of highly effective people: Powerful lessons in personal change*. Simon and Schuster.
3. *Jordan Peterson on self-help and political correctness* (2018) ABC, 13 March, 11:02. Available at: https://www.abc.net.au/7.30/jordan-peterson-on-self-help-and-political/9540754 (Accessed: 18 December 2021).

Chapter 19

1. Newport, C. (2016). *Deep work: Rules for focused success in a distracted world*. Hachette UK.
2. *Robbins, T. (no date). How to Focus Better. Available at:* https://www.tonyrobbins.com/how-to-focus/ (Accessed: 18 December 2021).
3. James, W. (2000) *The Principles of Psychology: Volume 1*. London: Dover Publication Inc.

Chapter 20

1. Aurelius, M. (2013). *Marcus Aurelius: Meditations, Books 1-6*. Oxford University Press.
2. Find out more about Feed America here: https://www.feedingamerica.org/about-us/partners/entertainment-council/tony-robbins

Chapter 21

1. Dahl, R. (2003). *The twits*. Dramatic Publishing.
2. Wilde, O. (2006). *The picture of dorian gray*. OUP Oxford.
3. Gianaros, P. J., Marsland, A. L., Kuan, D. C. H., Schirda, B. L., Jennings, J. R., Sheu, L. K., ... & Manuck, S. B. (2014). An inflammatory pathway links atherosclerotic cardiovascular disease risk to neural activity evoked by the cognitive regulation of emotion. *Biological psychiatry*, *75*(9), 738-745.
4. Jewel (2016) *Never Broken: Songs are only half the story*. New York: Blue Rider Press

Chapter 22

2. Pressfield, S. (2002). *The war of art: Break through the blocks and win your inner creative battles.* Black Irish Entertainment LLC.
3. Covey, S. R. (2004). *The 7 habits of highly effective people: Powerful lessons in personal change.* Simon and Schuster.
4. This quote is widely attributed to Leonardo Di Vinci. I cannot locate the original text from which the quote is taken.

Chapter 23

1. *Brené Brown: The Call to Courage* (2019) Directed by Sandra Restrepo [film] Netflix
2. Brown, B. (2012). *Daring greatly: How the courage to be vulnerable transforms the way we live, love, parent, and lead.* Penguin.

Chapter 24

1. Ferris, T. (2011) *The 4-Hour Work Week: Escape the 9-5, live anywhere and join the new rich.* London: Vermilion
2. For more on the hero's journey see: Campbell, J. (2008). *The hero with a thousand faces* (Vol. 17). New World Library.
3. McRaven, W. H. (2017). *Make Your Bed: Small things that can change your life and maybe the world.* Penguin UK.

4. Currey, M. (2013). *Daily rituals: How great minds make time, find inspiration, and get to work*. Pan Macmillan.
5. Rohn, J. (2017) *The Ultimate Jim Rohn Library. Narrated by Jim Rohn*. Available at: https://www.audible.co.uk/pd/The-Ultimate-Jim-Rohn-Library-Audiobook/B076PRHZSD (Accessed: 17 December 2021).

Chapter 25

1. Syrus, P., & Lyman, D. (1856). *The moral sayings of Publius Syrus, a Roman slave: from the Latin*. LE Bernard & Company.
2. Archilochus, Greek Soldier, 650 BC
3. Knight, B., & Hammel, B. (2013). *The power of negative thinking: An unconventional approach to achieving positive results*. Houghton Mifflin Harcourt.

Chapter 26

1. Tennyson, A. T. B. (1950). *Ulysses*. Chatto & Windus.
2. This famous Zen proverb is similar to the following quote taken from Marcus Aurelius' *'Meditations'*: "The impediment to action advances action. What stands in the way becomes the way."
3. Holiday, R. (2014). *The obstacle is the way: The ancient art of turning adversity to advantage.* Profile Books.
4. WIllink, J. (2015) *Jocko Podcast 3: Jocko & Echo (The Last Hundred Yards [book], Jiu Jitsu,*

Bosses, Failure) [Podcast]. 31 December.
Available at:
https://podcasts.apple.com/ie/podcast/jocko-podcast-3-jocko-echo-last-hundred-yards-book/id1070322219?i=1000364614945 (Accessed:
20 December 2021).

5. Disraeli, B. (1880). *Endymion* (Vol. 1). D. Appleton.

Chapter 27

1. Peterson, J. (2017) *Biblical Series XI: Sodom and Gomorrah. Available at:
https://www.youtube.com/watch?v=SKzpj0Ev8Xs&t=589s* (Accessed: 20 December 2021).
2. Keller, T. (1994) *Noah & the Reasons of Faith; Faith as Understanding.* [Podcast]. 18 September.
Available at:
https://gospelinlife.com/downloads/noah-and-the-reasons-of-faith-faith-as-understanding-6350/ (Accessed: 20 December 2021).
3. Emerson, R. W. (2020). *Self-reliance and other essays.* General Press.

Chapter 28

1. Nietzsche, F. (1990). *Twilight of idols and Anti-christ.* Penguin UK.
2. Sinek, S. (2009) *How great leaders inspire action.* Available at:
www.ted.com/talks/simon_sinek_how_great_leaders_inspire_action?language=en (Accessed: 20 December 2021).

3. This quote is widely attributed to Winston Churchill. I cannot locate the original text from which the quote is taken.

4. Success (2015) *John C. Maxwell: 5 Qualities of People Who Use Time Wisely*. Available at: https://www.success.com/john-c-maxwell-5-qualities-of-people-who-use-time-wisely/ (Accessed: 20 December 2021).

Chapter 29

1. Rogan, J. (2017) *#958 – Jordan Peterson.* [Podcast]. 9 May. Available at: https://open.spotify.com/episode/5194p3rIfeyMGbo8YKGMJK (Accessed: 20 December 2021).

2. Purdie, A. (2011) *Living Beyond Limits.* Available at: https://www.ted.com/talks/amy_purdy_living_beyond_limits (Accessed: 20 December 2021).

3. Robbins, T. (no date). *Dealing with Grief.* Available at: https://www.tonyrobbins.com/dealing-with-grief/ (Accessed: 18 December 2021).

Chapter 30

1. Angelou, M. (1997). *I know why the caged bird sings*. Bantam.

2. *The Hobbit: The Battle of the Five Armies* (2014) Directed by Jackson, P. [Feature film]. New Zealand: Warner Bros.

3. The Art of Manliness (2017) *Podcast #335: Exploring Archetypes With Jordan B. Peterson* [Podcast]. 31 August. Available at:

https://www.artofmanliness.com/character/advice/
podcast-335-using-power-myths-live-flourishing-
life/ (Accessed: 21 December 2021).

Chapter 31

1. Philippians 4: 8, Holy Bible. New International
   Version
2. Proverbs 24: 30 – 34, Holy Bible. New International
   Version

Chapter 32

1. Von Goethe, J. W., & Greenberg, M. (2014). *Faust*.
   Yale University Press.
   While this quote is taken from Faust there is an
   interesting story about how it came to be, you can
   read it here:
   https://quoteinvestigator.com/2016/02/09/boldnes
   s/
2. The notion that the fool is the precursor the saviour
   is widely attributed to Carl Jung; however, I cannot
   locate the original source for this quote, and as a
   result, wonder whether the quote represents a
   summary of Jungian idea presented by Prof. Jordan
   Peterson. You can listen to Prof. Peterson discuss
   this idea here:
   https://podcasts.apple.com/us/podcast/the-fool-
   precedes-the-
   master/id1462681901?i=1000462018403
3. Gilbert, E. (2016). *Big magic: Creative living beyond
   fear*. Penguin.

Chapter 33

1. Campbell, J. (2008). *The hero with a thousand faces* (Vol. 17). New World Library.
2. Tolkien, J. R. R. (2018). *The hobbit, or there and back again*. ARC, Amsterdam University Press.
3. Jung, C. G. (1971). Mysterium coniunctionis. The quote is a paraphrase of an old alchemical dictum "*In sterquiliniis invenitur*" - in filth it will be found.
4. Tolkien, J. R. R. (2012). *The lord of the rings: one volume*. Houghton Mifflin Harcourt.

Chapter 34

1. Angelou, M. (2012). *Letter to my daughter*. GagasMedia
2. Holiday, R. (2014). *The obstacle is the way: The ancient art of turning adversity to advantage*. Profile Books.
3. As quoted in *The Ring of Truth* (2004) by Joseph O'Day
4. This quote is widely attributed to Victor Hugo. I cannot locate the original text from which the quote is taken.

Chapter 35

1. Singer, M. (2007). *The untethered soul: The journey beyond yourself*. New Harbinger Publications.

2. Rogers, C. R. (1995). *On becoming a person: A therapist's view of psychotherapy*. Houghton Mifflin Harcourt.

Chapter 36

1. Aurelius, M. (2013). *Marcus Aurelius: Meditations, Books 1-6*. Oxford University Press.
2. Maltz, M. (2002). *New psycho-cybernetics*. Penguin.

Chapter 37

1. *Sister Act 2: Back in the Habit* (1993) Directed by Bill Duke [Feature Film]. United States: Buena Vista Pictures.
2. Schwarzenegger, A., & Petre, P. (2013). *Total Recall: My Unbelievably True Life Story*. Simon and Schuster.

Acknowledgements

Many people have helped me write this book. I was first inspired when listening to Tim Ferris and it seems only right that I acknowledge the role he played in getting me started.

The various authors that I've listed throughout this book have also played a key role in inspiring and motivating me to write. Their work has challenged my thinking and encouraged me to continue even when I felt my work wasn't good enough.

A number of friends have proofread my work and provided excellent feedback, most notably Hollie Morrison, whose expertise and insight were invaluable and Megan McUnipal, who was an encouraging voice throughout this process.

I would like to thank my beautiful wife Elizabeth, whose unconditional love, encouragement and deep thinking have helped me go from an idea to finished product. Thank you for loving me.

Lastly, to Jesus, who saved me.

"You make known to me the path of life."
~ Psalm 16:11 ~

AS A MAN THINKETH

BY

JAMES ALLEN

Author of "From Passion to Peace"

"Mind is the Master power that moulds and makes,

And Man is Mind, and evermore he takes

The tool of Thought, and, shaping what he wills,

Brings forth a thousand joys, a thousand ills:

He thinks in secret, and it comes to pass:

Environment is but his looking-glass."

Jonathan Brown

CONTENTS

FOREWORD

This little volume (the result of meditation and experience) is not intended as an exhaustive treatise on the much-written-upon subject of the power of thought. It is suggestive rather than explanatory, its object being to stimulate men and women to the discovery and perception of the truth that--

"They themselves are makers of themselves."

by virtue of the thoughts, which they choose and encourage; that mind is the master-weaver, both of the inner garment of character and the outer garment of circumstance, and that, as they may have hitherto woven in ignorance and pain they may now weave in enlightenment and happiness.

JAMES ALLEN.

BROAD PARK AVENUE,

ILFRACOMBE,

ENGLAND

AS A MAN THINKETH

THOUGHT AND CHARACTER

The aphorism, "As a man thinketh in his heart so is he," not only embraces the whole of a man's being, but is so comprehensive as to reach out to every condition and circumstance of his life. A man is literally _what he thinks, his character being the complete sum of all his thoughts.

As the plant springs from, and could not be without, the seed, so every act of a man springs from the hidden seeds of thought, and could not have appeared without them. This applies equally to those acts called "spontaneous" and "unpremeditated" as to those, which are deliberately executed.

Act is the blossom of thought, and joy and suffering are its fruits; thus does a man garner in the sweet and bitter fruitage of his own husbandry.

"Thought in the mind hath made us, what we are

By thought was wrought and built. If a man's mind

Hath evil thoughts, pain comes on him as comes

The wheel the ox behind....

..If one endure

In purity of thought, joy follows him

As his own shadow--sure."

Man is a growth by law, and not a creation by artifice, and cause and effect is as absolute and undeviating in the hidden realm of thought as in the world of visible and material things. A noble and Godlike character is not a thing of favour or chance, but is the natural result of continued effort in right thinking, the effect of long-cherished association with Godlike thoughts. An ignoble and bestial character, by the same process, is the result of the continued harbouring of grovelling thoughts.

Man is made or unmade by himself; in the armoury of thought he forges the weapons by which he destroys himself; he also fashions the tools with which he builds for himself heavenly mansions of joy and strength and peace. By the right choice and true application of thought, man ascends to the Divine Perfection; by the abuse and wrong application of thought, he descends below the level of the beast. Between these two extremes are all the grades of character, and man is their maker and master.

Of all the beautiful truths pertaining to the soul which have been restored and brought to light in this age, none is more gladdening or fruitful of divine promise and confidence than this--that man is the master of thought, the moulder of character, and the maker and shaper of condition, environment, and destiny.

As a being of Power, Intelligence, and Love, and the lord of his own thoughts, man holds the key to every situation, and contains within himself that transforming and regenerative agency by which he may make himself what he wills.

Man is always the master, even in his weaker and most abandoned state; but in his weakness and degradation he is the foolish master who misgoverns his "household." When he begins to reflect upon his

condition, and to search diligently for the Law upon which his being is established, he then becomes the wise master, directing his energies with intelligence, and fashioning his thoughts to fruitful issues. Such is the _conscious_ master, and man can only thus become by discovering _within himself_ the laws of thought; which discovery is totally a matter of application, self analysis, and experience.

Only by much searching and mining, are gold and diamonds obtained, and man can find every truth connected with his being, if he will dig deep into the mine of his soul; and that he is the maker of his character, the moulder of his life, and the builder of his destiny, he may unerringly prove, if he will watch, control, and alter his thoughts, tracing their effects upon himself, upon others, and upon his life and circumstances, linking cause and effect by patient practice and investigation, and utilizing his every experience, even to the most trivial, everyday occurrence, as a means of obtaining that knowledge of himself which is Understanding, Wisdom, Power. In this direction, as in no other, is the law absolute that "He that seeketh findeth; and to him that knocketh it shall be opened;" for only by patience, practice, and ceaseless importunity can a man enter the Door of the Temple of Knowledge.

EFFECT OF THOUGHT ON CIRCUMSTANCES

Man's mind may be likened to a garden, which may be intelligently cultivated or allowed to run wild; but whether cultivated or neglected, it must, and will, bring forth. If no useful seeds are put into it, then an abundance of useless weed-seeds will fall therein, and will continue to produce their kind.

Just as a gardener cultivates his plot, keeping it free from weeds, and growing the flowers and fruits which he requires, so may a man tend the garden of his mind, weeding out all the wrong, useless, and impure thoughts, and cultivating toward perfection the flowers and fruits of right, useful, and pure thoughts. By pursuing this process, a man sooner or later discovers that he is the master-gardener of his soul, the director of his life. He also reveals, within himself, the laws of thought, and understands, with ever-increasing accuracy, how the thought-forces and mind elements operate in the shaping of his character, circumstances, and destiny.

Thought and character are one, and as character can only manifest and discover itself through environment and circumstance, the outer conditions of a person's life will always be found to be harmoniously related to his inner state. This does not mean that a man's circumstances at any given time are an indication of his entire character, but that those circumstances are so intimately connected with some vital thought-element within himself that, for the time being, they are indispensable to his development.

Every man is where he is by the law of his being; the thoughts which he has built into his character have brought him there, and in the arrangement of his life there is no element of chance, but all is the result of a law which cannot err. This is just as true of those who feel "out of harmony" with their surroundings as of those who are contented with them.

As a progressive and evolving being, man is where he is that he may learn that he may grow; and as he learns the spiritual lesson which any circumstance contains for him, it passes away and gives place to other circumstances.

Man is buffeted by circumstances so long as he believes himself to be the creature of outside conditions, but when he realizes that he is a creative power, and that he may command the hidden soil and seeds of his being out of which circumstances grow, he then becomes the rightful master of himself.

That circumstances grow out of thought every man knows who has for any length of time practised self-control and self-purification, for he will have noticed that the alteration in his circumstances has been in exact ratio with his altered mental condition. So true is this that when a man earnestly applies himself to remedy the defects in his character, and makes swift and marked progress, he passes rapidly through a succession of vicissitudes.

The soul attracts that which it secretly harbours; that which it loves, and also that which it fears; it reaches the height of its cherished aspirations; it falls to the level of its unchastened desires, and circumstances are the means by which the soul receives its own.

Every thought-seed sown or allowed to fall into the mind, and to take root there, produces its own, blossoming sooner or later into act, and bearing its own fruitage of opportunity and circumstance.

Good thoughts bear good fruit, bad thoughts bad fruit.

The outer world of circumstance shapes itself to the inner world of thought, and both pleasant and unpleasant external conditions are factors, which make for the ultimate good of the individual. As the reaper of his own harvest, man learns both by suffering and bliss.

Following the inmost desires, aspirations, thoughts, by which he allows himself to be dominated, (pursuing the will-o'-the-wisps of impure imaginings or steadfastly walking the highway of strong and high endeavour), a man at last arrives at their fruition and fulfilment in the outer conditions of his life. The laws of growth and adjustment everywhere obtains.

A man does not come to the alms-house or the jail by the tyranny of fate or circumstance, but by the pathway of grovelling thoughts and base desires. Nor does a pure-minded man fall suddenly into crime by stress of any mere external force; the criminal thought had long been secretly fostered in the heart, and the hour of opportunity revealed its gathered power. Circumstance does not make the man; it reveals him to himself No such conditions can exist as descending into vice and its attendant sufferings apart from vicious inclinations, or ascending into virtue and its pure happiness without the continued cultivation of virtuous aspirations, and man, therefore, as the lord and master of thought, is the maker of himself the shaper and author of environment. Even at birth the soul comes to its own and through every step of its earthly pilgrimage it attracts those combinations of conditions which reveal itself, which are the reflections of its own purity and, impurity, its strength and weakness.

Men do not attract that which they want, but that which they are. Their whims, fancies, and ambitions are thwarted at every step, but their inmost thoughts and desires are fed with their own food, be it foul or clean. The "divinity that shapes our ends" is in ourselves; it is our very self. Only himself manacles man: thought and action are the gaolers of Fate--they imprison, being base; they are also the angels of Freedom--they liberate, being noble. Not what he wishes and prays for does a man get, but what he justly earns. His wishes and prayers are only gratified and answered when they harmonize with his thoughts and actions.

In the light of this truth, what, then, is the meaning of "fighting against circumstances?" It means that a man is continually revolting against an effect without, while all the time he is nourishing and preserving its cause in his heart. That cause may take the form of a conscious vice or an unconscious weakness; but whatever it is, it stubbornly retards the efforts of its possessor, and thus calls aloud for remedy.

Men are anxious to improve their circumstances, but are unwilling to improve themselves; they therefore remain bound. The man who does not shrink from self-crucifixion can never fail to accomplish the object upon which his heart is set. This is as true of earthly as of heavenly things. Even the man whose sole object is to acquire wealth must be prepared to make great personal sacrifices before he can accomplish his object; and how much more so he who would realize a strong and well-poised life?

Here is a man who is wretchedly poor. He is extremely anxious that his surroundings and home comforts should be improved, yet all the time he shirks his work, and considers he is justified in trying to deceive his employer on the ground of the insufficiency of his wages. Such a man does not understand the simplest rudiments of those principles which are the basis of true prosperity, and is not only totally unfitted to rise out of his wretchedness, but is actually attracting to himself a still deeper wretchedness by dwelling in, and acting out, indolent, deceptive, and unmanly thoughts.

Here is a rich man who is the victim of a painful and persistent disease as the result of gluttony. He is willing to give large sums of money to get rid of it, but he will not sacrifice his gluttonous desires. He wants to gratify his taste for rich and unnatural viands and have his health as well. Such a man is totally unfit to have health, because he has not yet learned the first principles of a healthy life.

Here is an employer of labour who adopts crooked measures to avoid paying the regulation wage, and, in the hope of making larger profits, reduces the wages of his workpeople. Such a man is altogether unfitted for prosperity, and when he finds himself bankrupt, both as regards reputation and riches, he blames circumstances, not knowing that he is the sole author of his condition.

I have introduced these three cases merely as illustrative of the truth that man is the causer (though nearly always is unconsciously) of his circumstances, and that, whilst aiming at a good end, he is continually frustrating its accomplishment by encouraging thoughts and desires which cannot possibly harmonize with that end. Such cases could be multiplied and varied almost indefinitely, but this is not necessary, as the reader can, if he so resolves, trace the action of the laws of thought in his own mind and life, and until this is done, mere external facts cannot serve as a ground of reasoning.

Circumstances, however, are so complicated, thought is so deeply rooted, and the conditions of happiness vary so, vastly with individuals, that a man's entire soul-condition (although it may be known to himself) cannot be judged by another from the external aspect of his life alone. A man may be honest in certain directions, yet suffer privations; a man may be dishonest in certain directions, yet acquire wealth; but the conclusion usually formed that the one man fails because of his particular honesty, and that the other prospers because of his particular dishonesty, is the result of a superficial judgment, which assumes that the dishonest man is almost totally corrupt, and the honest man almost entirely virtuous. In the light of a deeper knowledge and wider experience such judgment is found to be erroneous.

The dishonest man may have some admirable virtues, which the other does, not possess; and the honest man obnoxious vices which are absent in the other. The honest man reaps the good results of his honest thoughts and acts; he also brings upon himself the sufferings, which his vices produce. The dishonest man likewise garners his own suffering and happiness.

It is pleasing to human vanity to believe that one suffers because of one's virtue; but not until a man has extirpated every sickly, bitter, and impure thought from his mind, and washed every sinful

stain from his soul, can he be in a position to know and declare that his sufferings are the result of his good, and not of his bad qualities; and on the way to, yet long before he has reached, that supreme perfection, he will have found, working in his mind and life, the Great Law which is absolutely just, and which cannot, therefore, give good for evil, evil for good. Possessed of such knowledge, he will then know, looking back upon his past ignorance and blindness, that his life is, and always was, justly ordered, and that all his past experiences, good and bad, were the equitable outworking of his evolving, yet unevolved self.

Good thoughts and actions can never produce bad results; bad thoughts and actions can never produce good results. This is but saying that nothing can come from corn but corn, nothing from nettles but nettles. Men understand this law in the natural world, and work with it; but few understand it in the mental and moral world (though its operation there is just as simple and undeviating), and they, therefore, do not co-operate with it.

Suffering is always the effect of wrong thought in some direction. It is an indication that the individual is out of harmony with himself, with the Law of his being. The sole and supreme use of suffering is to purify, to burn out all that is useless and impure.

Suffering ceases for him who is pure. There could be no object in burning gold after the dross had been removed, and a perfectly pure and enlightened being could not suffer.

The circumstances, which a man encounters with suffering, are the result of his own mental in harmony. The circumstances, which a man encounters with blessedness, are the result of his own mental harmony. Blessedness, not material possessions, is the measure of right thought; wretchedness, not lack of material possessions, is the measure of wrong thought. A man may be cursed and rich; he may be blessed and poor. Blessedness and riches are only joined together when the riches are rightly and wisely used; and the poor man only descends into wretchedness when he regards his lot as a burden unjustly imposed.

Indigence and indulgence are the two extremes of wretchedness. They are both equally unnatural and the result of mental disorder. A man is not rightly conditioned until he is a happy, healthy, and prosperous being; and happiness, health, and prosperity are the result of a harmonious adjustment of the inner with the outer, of the man with his surroundings.

A man only begins to be a man when he ceases to whine and revile, and commences to search for the hidden justice which regulates his life. And as he adapts his mind to that regulating factor, he ceases to accuse others as the cause of his condition, and builds himself up in strong and noble thoughts; ceases to kick against circumstances, but begins to use them as aids to his more rapid progress, and as a means of discovering the hidden powers and possibilities within himself.

Law, not confusion, is the dominating principle in the universe; justice, not injustice, is the soul and substance of life; and righteousness, not corruption, is the moulding and moving force in the spiritual government of the world. This being so, man has but to right himself to find that the universe is right; and during the process of putting himself right he will find that as he alters his thoughts towards things and other people, things and other people will alter towards him.

The proof of this truth is in every person, and it therefore admits of easy investigation by systematic introspection and self-analysis. Let a man radically alter his thoughts, and he will be astonished at the rapid transformation it will effect in the material conditions of his life. Men imagine that thought can be kept secret, but it cannot; it rapidly crystallizes into habit, and habit solidifies into circumstance. Bestial thoughts crystallize into habits of drunkenness and sensuality, which solidify into circumstances of destitution and disease: impure thoughts of every kind crystallize into enervating and confusing habits, which solidify into distracting and adverse circumstances: thoughts of fear, doubt, and indecision crystallize into weak, unmanly, and irresolute habits, which solidify into circumstances of failure, indigence, and slavish dependence: lazy thoughts crystallize into habits of uncleanliness and dishonesty, which solidify into circumstances of foulness and beggary: hateful and condemnatory thoughts crystallize into habits of accusation and violence, which solidify into circumstances of injury and persecution: selfish thoughts of all kinds crystallize into habits of self-seeking, which solidify into circumstances more or less distressing. On the other hand, beautiful thoughts of all kinds crystallize into habits of grace and kindliness, which solidify into genial and sunny circumstances: pure thoughts crystallize into habits of temperance and self-control, which solidify into circumstances of repose and peace: thoughts of courage, self-reliance, and decision crystallize into manly habits, which solidify into circumstances of success, plenty, and freedom: energetic thoughts crystallize into habits of cleanliness and industry, which solidify into circumstances of pleasantness: gentle and forgiving thoughts crystallize into habits of gentleness, which solidify into protective and preservative circumstances: loving and unselfish thoughts crystallize into habits of self-forgetfulness for others, which solidify into circumstances of sure and abiding prosperity and true riches.

A particular train of thought persisted in, be it good or bad, cannot fail to produce its results on the character and circumstances. A man cannot directly choose his circumstances, but he can choose his thoughts, and so indirectly, yet surely, shape his circumstances.

Nature helps every man to the gratification of the thoughts, which he most encourages, and opportunities are presented which will most speedily bring to the surface both the good and evil thoughts.

Let a man cease from his sinful thoughts, and all the world will soften towards him, and be ready to help him; let him put away his weakly and sickly thoughts, and lo, opportunities will spring up on every hand to aid his strong resolves; let him encourage good thoughts, and no hard fate shall bind him down to wretchedness and shame. The world is your kaleidoscope, and the varying combinations of colours, which at every succeeding moment it presents to you are the exquisitely adjusted pictures of your ever-moving thoughts.

"So You will be what you will to be;

Let failure find its false content

In that poor word, 'environment,'

But spirit scorns it, and is free.

"It masters time, it conquers space;

It cowes that boastful trickster, Chance,

And bids the tyrant Circumstance

Uncrown, and fill a servant's place.

"The human Will, that force unseen,

The offspring of a deathless Soul,

Can hew a way to any goal,

Though walls of granite intervene.

"Be not impatient in delays

But wait as one who understands;

When spirit rises and commands

The gods are ready to obey."

EFFECT OF THOUGHT ON HEALTH AND THE BODY

The body is the servant of the mind. It obeys the operations of the mind, whether they be deliberately chosen or automatically expressed. At the bidding of unlawful thoughts the body sinks rapidly into disease and decay; at the command of glad and beautiful thoughts it becomes clothed with youthfulness and beauty.

Disease and health, like circumstances, are rooted in thought. Sickly thoughts will express themselves through a sickly body. Thoughts of fear have been known to kill a man as speedily as a bullet, and they are continually killing thousands of people just as surely though less rapidly. The people who live in fear of disease are the people who get it. Anxiety quickly demoralizes the whole body, and lays it open to the entrance of disease; while impure thoughts, even if not physically indulged, will soon shatter the nervous system.

Strong, pure, and happy thoughts build up the body in vigour and grace. The body is a delicate and plastic instrument, which responds readily to the thoughts by which it is impressed, and habits of thought will produce their own effects, good or bad, upon it.

Men will continue to have impure and poisoned blood, so long as they propagate unclean thoughts. Out of a clean heart comes a clean life and a clean body. Out of a defiled mind proceeds a defiled life and a corrupt body. Thought is the fount of action, life, and manifestation; make the fountain pure, and all will be pure.

Change of diet will not help a man who will not change his thoughts. When a man makes his thoughts pure, he no longer desires impure food.

Clean thoughts make clean habits. The so-called saint who does not wash his body is not a saint. He who has strengthened and purified his thoughts does not need to consider the malevolent microbe.

If you would protect your body, guard your mind. If you would renew your body, beautify your mind. Thoughts of malice, envy, disappointment, despondency, rob the body of its health and grace. A sour face does not come by chance; it is made by sour thoughts. Wrinkles that mar are drawn by folly, passion, and pride.

I know a woman of ninety-six who has the bright, innocent face of a girl. I know a man well under middle age whose face is drawn into inharmonious contours. The one is the result of a sweet and sunny disposition; the other is the outcome of passion and discontent.

As you cannot have a sweet and wholesome abode unless you admit the air and sunshine freely into your rooms, so a strong body and a bright, happy, or serene countenance can only result from the free admittance into the mind of thoughts of joy and goodwill and serenity.

On the faces of the aged there are wrinkles made by sympathy, others by strong and pure thought, and others are carved by passion: who cannot distinguish them? With those who have lived righteously, age is calm, peaceful, and softly mellowed, like the setting sun. I have recently seen a philosopher on his deathbed. He was not old except in years. He died as sweetly and peacefully as he had lived.

There is no physician like cheerful thought for dissipating the ills of the body; there is no comforter to compare with goodwill for dispersing the shadows of grief and sorrow. To live continually in thoughts of ill will, cynicism, suspicion, and envy, is to be confined in a self made prison-hole. But to think well of all, to be cheerful with all, to patiently learn to find the good in all such unselfish thoughts are the very portals of heaven; and to dwell day by day in thoughts of peace toward every creature will bring abounding peace to their possessor.

THOUGHT AND PURPOSE

Until thought is linked with purpose there is no intelligent accomplishment. With the majority the bark of thought is allowed to "drift" upon the ocean of life. Aimlessness is a vice, and such drifting must not continue for him who would steer clear of catastrophe and destruction.

They who have no central purpose in their life fall an easy prey to petty worries, fears, troubles, and self-pity, all of which are indications of weakness, which lead, just as surely as deliberately planned sins (though by a different route), to failure, unhappiness, and loss, for weakness cannot persist in a power evolving universe.

A man should conceive of a legitimate purpose in his heart, and set out to accomplish it. He should make this purpose the centralizing point of his thoughts. It may take the form of a spiritual ideal, or it may be a worldly object, according to his nature at the time being; but whichever it is, he should steadily focus his thought-forces upon the object, which he has set before him. He should make this purpose his supreme duty, and should devote himself to its attainment, not allowing his thoughts to wander away into ephemeral fancies, longings, and imaginings. This is the royal road to self-control and true concentration of thought. Even if he fails again and again to accomplish his purpose (as he necessarily must until weakness is overcome), the strength of character gained will be the measure of his true success, and this will form a new starting-point for future power and triumph.

Those who are not prepared for the apprehension of a great purpose should fix the thoughts upon the faultless performance of their duty, no matter how insignificant their task may appear. Only in this way can the thoughts be gathered and focussed, and resolution and energy be developed, which being done, there is nothing which may not be accomplished.

The weakest soul, knowing its own weakness, and believing this truth that strength can only be developed by effort and practice, will, thus believing, at once begin to exert itself, and, adding effort to effort, patience to patience, and strength to strength, will never cease to develop, and will at last grow divinely strong.

As the physically weak man can make himself strong by careful and patient training, so the man of weak thoughts can make them strong by exercising himself in right thinking.

To put away aimlessness and weakness, and to begin to think with purpose, is to enter the ranks of those strong ones who only recognize failure as one of the pathways to attainment; who make all conditions serve them, and who think strongly, attempt fearlessly, and accomplish masterfully.

Having conceived of his purpose, a man should mentally mark out a straight pathway to its achievement, looking neither to the right nor the left. Doubts and fears should be rigorously excluded; they are disintegrating elements, which break up the straight line of effort, rendering it crooked, ineffectual, useless. Thoughts of doubt and fear never accomplished anything, and never can. They always lead to failure. Purpose, energy, power to do, and all strong thoughts cease when doubt and fear creep in.

The will to do springs from the knowledge that we can do. Doubt and fear are the great enemies of knowledge, and he who encourages them, who does not slay them, thwarts himself at every step.

He who has conquered doubt and fear has conquered failure. His every thought is allied with power, and all difficulties are bravely met and wisely overcome. His purposes are seasonably planted, and they bloom and bring forth fruit, which does not fall prematurely to the ground.

Thought allied fearlessly to purpose becomes creative force: he who knows this is ready to become something higher and stronger than a mere bundle of wavering thoughts and fluctuating sensations; he who does this has become the conscious and intelligent wielder of his mental powers.

THE THOUGHT-FACTOR IN ACHIEVEMENT

All that a man achieves and all that he fails to achieve is the direct result of his own thoughts. In a justly ordered universe, where loss of equipoise would mean total destruction, individual responsibility must be absolute. A man's weakness and strength, purity and impurity, are his own, and not another man's; they are brought about by himself, and not by another; and they can only be altered by himself, never by another. His condition is also his own, and not another man's. His suffering and his happiness are evolved from within. As he thinks, so he is; as he continues to think, so he remains.

A strong man cannot help a weaker unless that weaker is willing to be helped, and even then the weak man must become strong of himself; he must, by his own efforts, develop the strength which he admires in another. None but himself can alter his condition.

It has been usual for men to think and to say, "Many men are slaves because one is an oppressor; let us hate the oppressor." Now, however, there is amongst an increasing few a tendency to reverse this judgment, and to say, "One man is an oppressor because many are slaves; let us despise the slaves."

The truth is that oppressor and slave are co-operators in ignorance, and, while seeming to afflict each other, are in reality afflicting themselves. A perfect Knowledge perceives the action of law in the weakness of the oppressed and the misapplied power of the oppressor; a perfect Love, seeing the suffering, which both states entail, condemns neither; a perfect Compassion embraces both oppressor and oppressed.

He who has conquered weakness, and has put away all selfish thoughts, belongs neither to oppressor nor oppressed. He is free.

A man can only rise, conquer, and achieve by lifting up his thoughts. He can only remain weak, and abject, and miserable by refusing to lift up his thoughts.

Before a man can achieve anything, even in worldly things, he must lift his thoughts above slavish animal indulgence. He may not, in order to succeed, give up all animality and selfishness, by any means; but a portion of it must, at least, be sacrificed. A man whose first thought is bestial indulgence could neither think clearly nor plan methodically; he could not find and develop his latent resources, and would fail in any undertaking. Not having commenced to manfully control his thoughts, he is not in a position to control affairs and to adopt serious responsibilities. He is not fit to act independently and stand alone. But he is limited only by the thoughts, which he chooses.

There can be no progress, no achievement without sacrifice, and a man's worldly success will be in the measure that he sacrifices his confused animal thoughts, and fixes his mind on the development of his plans, and the strengthening of his resolution and self-reliance. And the higher he lifts his thoughts, the more manly, upright, and righteous he becomes, the greater will be his success, the more blessed and enduring will be his achievements.

The universe does not favour the greedy, the dishonest, the vicious, although on the mere surface it may sometimes appear to do so; it helps the honest, the magnanimous, the virtuous. All the great

Teachers of the ages have declared this in varying forms, and to prove and know it a man has but to persist in making himself more and more virtuous by lifting up his thoughts.

Intellectual achievements are the result of thought consecrated to the search for knowledge, or for the beautiful and true in life and nature. Such achievements may be sometimes connected with vanity and ambition, but they are not the outcome of those characteristics; they are the natural outgrowth of long and arduous effort, and of pure and unselfish thoughts.

Spiritual achievements are the consummation of holy aspirations. He who lives constantly in the conception of noble and lofty thoughts, who dwells upon all that is pure and unselfish, will, as surely as the sun reaches its zenith and the moon its full, become wise and noble in character, and rise into a position of influence and blessedness.

Achievement, of whatever kind, is the crown of effort, the diadem of thought. By the aid of self-control, resolution, purity, righteousness, and well-directed thought a man ascends; by the aid of animality, indolence, impurity, corruption, and confusion of thought a man descends.

A man may rise to high success in the world, and even to lofty altitudes in the spiritual realm, and again descend into weakness and wretchedness by allowing arrogant, selfish, and corrupt thoughts to take possession of him.

Victories attained by right thought can only be maintained by watchfulness. Many give way when success is assured, and rapidly fall back into failure.

All achievements, whether in the business, intellectual, or spiritual world, are the result of definitely directed thought, are governed by the same law and are of the same method; the only difference lies in the object of attainment.

He who would accomplish little must sacrifice little; he who would achieve much must sacrifice much; he who would attain highly must sacrifice greatly.

VISIONS AND IDEALS

The dreamers are the saviours of the world. As the visible world is sustained by the invisible, so men, through all their trials and sins and sordid vocations, are nourished by the beautiful visions of their solitary dreamers. Humanity cannot forget its dreamers; it cannot let their ideals fade and die; it lives in them; it knows them as the realities which it shall one day see and know.

Composer, sculptor, painter, poet, prophet, sage, these are the makers of the after-world, the architects of heaven. The world is beautiful because they have lived; without them, labouring humanity would perish.

He who cherishes a beautiful vision, a lofty ideal in his heart, will one day realize it. Columbus cherished a vision of another world, and he discovered it; Copernicus fostered the vision of a multiplicity of worlds and a wider universe, and he revealed it;

Buddha beheld the vision of a spiritual world of stainless beauty and perfect peace, and he entered into it.

Cherish your visions; cherish your ideals; cherish the music that stirs in your heart, the beauty that forms in your mind, the loveliness that drapes your purest thoughts, for out of them will grow all delightful conditions, all, heavenly environment; of these, if you but remain true to them, your world will at last be built.

To desire is to obtain; to aspire is to, achieve. Shall man's basest desires receive the fullest measure of gratification, and his purest aspirations starve for lack of sustenance? Such is not the Law: such a condition of things can never obtain: "ask and receive."

Dream lofty dreams, and as you dream, so shall you become. Your Vision is the promise of what you shall one day be; your Ideal is the prophecy of what you shall at last unveil.

The greatest achievement was at first and for a time a dream. The oak sleeps in the acorn; the bird waits in the egg;

and in the highest vision of the soul a waking angel stirs. Dreams are the seedlings of realities.

Your circumstances may be uncongenial, but they shall not long remain so if you but perceive an Ideal and strive to reach it. You cannot travel within and stand still without. Here is a youth hard pressed by poverty and labour; confined long hours in an unhealthy workshop; unschooled, and lacking all the arts of refinement. But he dreams of better things; he thinks of intelligence, of refinement, of grace and beauty. He conceives of, mentally builds up, an ideal condition of life; the vision of a wider liberty and a larger scope takes possession of him; unrest urges him to action, and he utilizes all his spare time and means, small though they are, to the development of his latent powers and resources. Very soon so altered has his mind become that the workshop can no longer hold him. It has become so out of harmony with his mentality that it falls out of his life as a garment is cast aside, and, with the growth of opportunities, which fit the scope of his expanding powers, he passes out of it forever. Years later we see this youth as a full-grown man. We find him a master of certain forces of the mind, which he wields with worldwide influence and almost unequalled power. In his hands he holds the cords of gigantic responsibilities; he speaks, and lo, lives are changed; men and women hang upon his words and remould their characters, and, sunlike, he becomes the fixed and luminous centre round which innumerable destinies revolve. He has realized the Vision of his youth. He has become one with his Ideal.

And you, too, youthful reader, will realize the Vision (not the idle wish) of your heart, be it base or beautiful, or a mixture of both, for you will always gravitate toward that which you, secretly, most love. Into your hands will be placed the exact results of your own thoughts; you will receive that which you earn; no more, no less. Whatever your present environment may be, you will fall, remain, or rise with your thoughts, your Vision, your Ideal. You will become as small as your controlling desire; as great as your dominant aspiration: in the beautiful words of Stanton Kirkham Davis, "You may be keeping accounts, and presently you shall walk out of the door that for so long has seemed to you the barrier of your ideals, and shall find yourself before an audience--the pen still behind your ear, the ink stains on your fingers and then and there shall pour out the torrent of your inspiration. You may be driving sheep, and you shall wander to the city-bucolic and open-mouthed; shall wander under the intrepid guidance of the spirit into the studio of the master, and after a time he shall say, 'I have nothing more to teach you.' And now you have become the master, who did so recently dream of great things while driving sheep. You shall lay down the saw and the plane to take upon yourself the regeneration of the world."

The thoughtless, the ignorant, and the indolent, seeing only the apparent effects of things and not the things themselves, talk of luck, of fortune, and chance. Seeing a man grow rich, they say, "How lucky he is!" Observing another become intellectual, they exclaim, "How highly favoured he is!" And noting the saintly character and wide influence of another, they remark, "How chance aids him at every turn!" They do not see the trials and failures and struggles which these men have voluntarily encountered in order to gain their experience; have no knowledge of the sacrifices they have made, of the undaunted efforts they have put forth, of the faith they have exercised, that they might overcome the apparently insurmountable, and realize the Vision of their heart. They do not know the darkness and the heartaches; they only see the light and joy, and call it "luck". They do not see the long and arduous journey, but only behold the pleasant goal, and call it "good fortune," do not understand the process, but only perceive the result, and call it chance.

In all human affairs there are efforts, and there are results, and the strength of the effort is the measure of the result. Chance is not. Gifts, powers, material, intellectual, and spiritual possessions are the fruits of effort; they are thoughts completed, objects accomplished, visions realized.

The Vision that you glorify in your mind, the Ideal that you enthrone in your heart--this you will build your life by, this you will become.

SERENITY

Calmness of mind is one of the beautiful jewels of wisdom. It is the result of long and patient effort in self-control. Its presence is an indication of ripened experience, and of a more than ordinary knowledge of the laws and operations of thought.

A man becomes calm in the measure that he understands himself as a thought evolved being, for such knowledge necessitates the understanding of others as the result of thought, and as he develops a right understanding, and sees more and more clearly the internal relations of things by the action of cause and effect he ceases to fuss and fume and worry and grieve, and remains poised, steadfast, serene.

The calm man, having learned how to govern himself, knows how to adapt himself to others; and they, in turn, reverence his spiritual strength, and feel that they can learn of him and rely upon him. The more tranquil a man becomes, the greater is his success, his influence, his power for good. Even the ordinary trader will find his business prosperity increase as he develops a greater self-control and equanimity, for people will always prefer to deal with a man whose demeanour is strongly equable.

The strong, calm man is always loved and revered. He is like a shade-giving tree in a thirsty land, or a sheltering rock in a storm. "Who does not love a tranquil heart, a sweet-tempered, balanced life? It does not matter whether it rains or shines, or what changes come to those possessing these blessings, for they are always sweet, serene, and calm. That exquisite poise of character, which we call serenity is the last lesson of culture, the fruitage of the soul. It is precious as wisdom, more to be desired than gold--yea, than even fine gold. How insignificant mere money seeking looks in comparison with a serene life--a life that dwells in the ocean of Truth, beneath the waves, beyond the reach of tempests, in the Eternal Calm!

"How many people we know who sour their lives, who ruin all that is sweet and beautiful by explosive tempers, who destroy their poise of character, and make bad blood! It is a question whether the great majority of people do not ruin their lives and mar their happiness by lack of self-control. How few people we meet in life who are well balanced, who have that exquisite poise which is characteristic of the finished character!

Yes, humanity surges with uncontrolled passion, is tumultuous with ungoverned grief, is blown about by anxiety and doubt only the wise man, only he whose thoughts are controlled and purified, makes the winds and the storms of the soul obey him.

Tempest-tossed souls, wherever ye may be, under whatsoever conditions ye may live, know this in the ocean of life the isles of Blessedness are smiling, and the sunny shore of your ideal awaits your coming. Keep your hand firmly upon the helm of thought. In the bark of your soul reclines the commanding Master; He does but sleep: wake Him. Self-control is strength; Right Thought is mastery; Calmness is power. Say unto your heart, "Peace, be still!"

Printed in Great Britain
by Amazon

20133125R00142